Dakini Teachings

Dakini Teachings

PADMASAMBHAVA'S
ORAL INSTRUCTIONS
TO LADY TSOGYAL

Recorded and concealed by YESHE TSOGYAL
Revealed by NYANG RAL NYIMA ÖSER
and SANGYE LINGPA

Translated according the oral teachings
of Kyabje Tulku Urgyen Rinpoche
by ERIK PEMA KUNSANG

RANGJUNG YESHE
PUBLICATIONS
BOUDHANATH, HONG KONG & ESBY
1999

RANGJUNG YESHE PUBLICATIONS
Flat 5a, Greenview Garden,
125 Robinson Road, Hong Kong

Address letters to:
Rangjung Yeshe Publications
P.O. Box 1200,
Kathmandu, Nepal

www.rangjung.com

Distributed to the book trade by North Atlantic Books
and Random House.

PUBLICATION DATA:

Dakini Teachings: Padmasambhava's Oral Instructions
to Lady Tsogyal. From the revelations of Nyang Ral Nyima Özer, Sangye
Lingpa and Dorje Lingpa.
Translated from the Tibetan according to the teachings of
Kyabje Tulku Urgyen Rinpoche by Erik Pema Kunsang
(Erik Hein Schmidt). Edited by Marcia Binder Schmidt.

TIBETAN TITLES:
Jo mo la gdams pa'i skor, jo mo zhu lan, mnga' bdag myang gi dmar khrid, bla
ma dgongs 'dus las mtsho rgyal zhu lan, rdo rje gling pa'i mar gyi yang zhun.

ISBN 978–962-7341-36-9 (pbk.)

1. Dakini Teachings, Vol. I. 2. Eastern philosophy — Buddhism.
3. Vajrayana — Tibet. I. Title. II. Padmasambhava (8th Cent.).
III. Ye shes mtsho rgyal (8th Cent.). IV. Myang ral nyi ma'i 'od zer
(1124-1182). V. Sangs rgyas gling pa (1340-1396). VI. rDo rje gling pa
(1346-1405).

COVER ART: Tibetan painting of Yeshe Tsogyal
Courtesy of Kunzang Choling

"Descend with the view while ascending with the conduct. It is most essential to practice these two as a unity."

—PADMASAMBHAVA

Contents

Translator's Preface   ix

A Short Biography of Padmasambhava
   by JAMGON KONGTRUL THE FIRST   xv

Introductory Teaching by VEN. TULKU URGYEN RINPOCHE   xxv

First of All   1

Taking Refuge   10

Bodhicitta   29

The Ten Foundations of Secret Mantra   59

The Vajra Master and the Yidam Deity   101

Vajrayana Mind Training   113

The Crystal Garland of Faultless Practice   135

The Refined Essence of Oral Instructions   153

Glossary   159

Translator's Preface

Dakini Teachings is a collection of advice selected from several revealed "treasure teachings," or *terma*. It contains Guru Rinpoche's (Padmasambhava's) oral instructions on Dharma practice given during his stay in Tibet in the ninth century. This advice was recorded by his chief disciple, the dakini Yeshe Tsogyal, the princess of Kharchen. According to Jamgon Kongtrul the First's *Lives of One Hundred Tertons,*[1] Yeshe Tsogyal was a dakini and an emanation of the female buddha Lochana, the consort of Buddha Ratnasambhava, as well as of Vajra Yogini appearing in the form of a woman. She served Guru Rinpoche during his stay in Tibet and afterward practiced with tremendous perseverance so that she finally became equal to Guru Rinpoche himself. Her compassion is matchless and her blessings are unceasing.

Yeshe Tsogyal wrote these oral instructions down in a secret code language called "dakini script" and concealed them as precious terma treasures to be revealed by tertons many centuries later. Guru Rinpoche himself predicted the arrival, names, and periods of the revealers. The teachings they would receive, in actuality or in visions, would be appropriate for the people in their own and in following generations. Almost every chapter in this book mentions that these teachings were given for the benefit of practitioners of future generations and includes the words: "May this meet with all worthy and destined people in the future!"

Dakini Teachings is based on the revealed termas of the twelfth-

---

1. Also called *The Precious Garland of Lapis Lazuli.*

century terton Nyang Ral Nyima Oser. The manuscripts that I have used were kept in the Royal Danish Library, having been brought back from a Mongolian monastery by an explorer of central Asia many decades ago. When His Holiness Dilgo Khyentse visited the library in 1976, he asked to be shown all the original handwritten manuscripts and decided to have photocopies made of six volumes of books that were unavailable at that time in India. Among these six was a collection of some of Nyang Ral's termas called *Jomo Shulen,* "The Questions and Answers of the Lady" (Tsogyal). This volume was later reprinted in its original form by Sherab Drimey, His Holiness Dilgo Khyentse's printer in New Delhi. When later I presented Ven. Tulku Urgyen Rinpoche with the book, he expressed great delight in reading it and gave me much encouragement in preparing this translation. He also pointed out another similar collection of Nyang Ral's termas called *Nyang-gyi Martri,* "The Direct Instructions of Nyang." Jamgon Kongtrul had found this text important enough to include in the sixtieth volume of the *Rinchen Terdzo.* In comparing these two manuscripts, I found that both contained invaluable advice by Padmasambhava that was sometimes identical and sometimes totally different. They were obviously from two entirely different sources, the first of which had not been available to Jamgon Kongtrul when preparing the *Rinchen Terdzo.*

It is now about eight hundred years since Nyang Ral Nyima Oser lived, and over these many years quite a few omissions and spelling mistakes crept in each time the manuscripts were hand copied. Even the mistakes were not the same in the two versions. Therefore I relied on a third collection of termas by the fourteenth-century master Sangye Lingpa. Parts of this collection were almost identical in wording with the terma of Nyang Ral Nyima Oser. The reason for the duplication is that both masters, in their former lives, were present when Guru Rinpoche gave the teaching. Nyang Ral Nyima Oser was the reincarnation of King Trisong Deutsen, and Sangye Lingpa was the reincarnation of Trisong Deutsen's second son, Murub Tseypo. There was enough material in these three collections to fill four additional books of English translation, so I selected what seemed to be most appropriate for the present day and age.

The following short biographical notes about the life of Nyang Ral Nyima Oser (1124–1192) are extracted from *The Lives of One Hundred Tertons*.

Nyang Ral is considered the first of the five terton kings prophesied by Guru Rinpoche. He was a reincarnation of Trisong Deutsen, the king who initially invited Guru Rinpoche to Tibet and who was also known as Tsangpa Lhai Metok (Divine Flower of Brahma).

He was born in the area of Lhodrak, the son of the Nyingma lama Nyangton Chokyi Khorlo, in the year of the Male Wood Dragon.[2]

At the age of eight he had visions of Buddha Shakyamuni, Avalokiteshvara, and Guru Rinpoche. His experience blazed forth for a whole month.

One evening he saw Guru Rinpoche riding a white horse carried by the four classes of dakinis and received the four empowerments by drinking nectar from Guru Rinpoche's vase. Upon receiving the empowerments he had the experience of the sky breaking open and the earth and mountains trembling, and he started to act in various strange ways to such an extent that everyone thought he had gone insane.

His father then gave him the empowerment of Hayagriva, and after practicing in retreat he had a vision of the deity and his phurba dagger emitted the neigh of a horse and he left imprints of his hands and feet in solid rock.

In accordance with a prediction from the dakinis, he went to Mawo Choqi Draktsa, where he was given the name Nyima Oser (Beam of Sunlight) by the wisdom dakinis. After this he was renowned under that name.

Guru Rinpoche appeared to Nyang Ral Nyima Oser in person and gave him the lists of termas he was to reveal. Accordingly, he revealed many volumes of terma teachings, among which the best known is the *Kagye Desheg Dupa,* a cycle of teachings focusing on the eight heruka sadhanas, and his revealed biography of Guru Rinpoche, known as *Sanglingma.*

---

2. The same year that Phadampa Sangye passed away.

He later married Jobum, an emanation of Yeshe Tsogyal, and had two sons, Drogon Namkha O and Namkha Pal, who both became lineage holders.

During his life he maintained a balance between practicing in retreat and teaching others. His activity stretched to the corners of the world and had a tremendous impact on the continuation of the Dharma.

In the year of the Male Wood Mouse he passed away at the age of sixty-nine, accompanied by many wonderful signs.

I, Jamgon Kongtrul, personally gathered all the transmissions for Nyang Ral's terma teachings, had the wood blocks carved for the nine volumes of *Kagye Desheg Dupa,* and performed its group sadhana many times. In that way I was able to offer my humble service to these teachings.

Here is some information describing how Nyima Oser received the actual terma from which the *Dakini Teachings* is taken, extracted from his biography called *The Clear Mirror,* which is found in the second volume of *Kagye Desheg Dupa.*

Later, when I stayed in retreat practicing guru sadhana at the Pear Crystal Cave of Pama Gong, one evening a white girl appeared and said she was Yeshe Tsogyal. She wore a blue dress with an apron and a shirt of white silk and said, "Yogi, what do you want?"

"I want nothing but the Dharma!" I replied.

"Then I will give you that," she said, and she handed me a casket with the scriptures of prophecies of the dakinis as well as the 108 cycles of questions and answers.

Then she said, "Son, come with me to the Sitavana charnel ground! Acharya Padma and the eight great vidyadharas as well as numerous other worthy yogis are holding a great Dharma assembly. We, the dakinis, are holding a great feast gathering, so come!"

We went there and I saw the great charnel ground; it was intimidating and frightening and impossible for unworthy people to approach. In the center sat a yogi with light brown skin on a huge throne made out of precious stones. He said, "Isn't that my son, Tsangpa Lhai Metok? Has wandering in samsara been a strain for you?" He told me then to sit down on a heap of human bones. I sat down.

In front of him there was a big mandala adorned with numerous ornaments encircled by a latticework of light rays. In the eight directions around it I saw that the eight vidyadharas of India and Tibet sat with smiling faces. I was overjoyed.

Then the same girl asked me, "Son, do you want to enjoy a feast gathering or the wheel of Dharma?" In reply I said, "Please turn the wheel of Dharma for me." Immediately, I was given the preliminary steps for initiation into this great mandala, after which I went to the mandala's eight directions, where each of the masters conferred upon me the extensive empowerments for each of the eight teachings and entrusted me with the lineage.

The yogi in the center, who said he was Padmasambhava, also known as Padmakara, gave me the great empowerment of the Assemblage of the Peaceful and Wrathful Sugatas. He also gave me the books and taught me the melodies for the chanting.

All the vidyadharas then simultaneously gave the empowerment for learning and retaining, the empowerment for meditating and practicing, the empowerment for explaining and teaching, the empowerment for taming beings through the activities, the empowerment for the all-encompassing command of a vajra king, and the Dzogchen empowerment for the expression of awareness.

Having received all these empowerments in their entirety, I was given a white conch and told to return home. The very moment I heard that, the whole scenery of the charnel ground and all the masters vanished just like vapor disappearing from a mirror. When I regained my senses, I found that I was back in my meditation hut.

The second terma that I used for comparison for clearing up the spelling mistakes and omissions when preparing *Dakini Teachings* was revealed by Sangye Lingpa (1340–1396). He took birth in Kongpo, the southeastern province of Tibet, in the year of the Male Iron Dragon, the same year that the fourth karmapa, Rolpey Dorje, was born. Sangye Lingpa is regarded as an incarnation of Yeshe Rolpa

Tsal, the second son of King Trisong Deutsen. In 1364 he revealed the Lama Gongdue cycle of teachings, his most important terma. Sangye Lingpa is also counted among the five terton kings. In recent times these two great masters were reborn as Jamyang Khyentse Wangpo and Terchen Chokgyur Lingpa.

Lastly, *Dakini Teachings* finishes with a chapter by the terton Guru Dorje Lingpa containing the last words of Padmasambhava. Dorje Lingpa (1346–1405) was one of five major revealers of hidden treasures in Tibet renowned as the five terton kings.

I would like to thank everyone who contributed to the preparation of this book, especially His Holiness Dilgo Khyentse and Ven. Tulku Urgyen Rinpoche for the directions and blessings. Marcia Binder Schmidt for rechecking the translation and overseeing the work at all stages, Mim Coulstock for editing, and Phinjo Sherpa for word-processing assistance.

This book contains some of the essence of Padmakara's oral instructions on general Dharma practice and on how to behave in a personal and realistic way. I am delighted that these precious teachings are now appearing in the English language. Although our translation may not be perfect in scholarship and literary eloquence, I believe that the link between Guru Rinpoche's blessings and the reader's openness and sincerity will make up for these shortcomings. Reading or listening to someone else read the *Dakini Teachings* will then be close to being in the presence of Guru Rinpoche. Just as these teachings have touched me, may they touch the hearts of many other people and be a continual source of inspiration.

ERIK PEMA KUNSANG
Asura Cave, 1989

A Short Biography of Padmasambhava

by JAMGON KONGTRUL THE FIRST

This short life story of Padmasambhava, also known as Guru Rinpoche or Padmakara, is extracted from The Precious Garland of Lapis Lazuli, *a collection of life stories of the 108 main tertons written by Jamgon Kongtrul the First and found in volume 1 of his* Rinchen Terdzo.

Padmakara has influenced countless beings through the Vajrayana teachings and in particular through the activity of the profound terma treasures. This great master was not an ordinary person on the path or just a noble being on one of the bodhisattva bhumis but an emanation of both Buddha Amitabha and Shakyamuni who appeared in order to tame the human beings and spirits who are difficult to convert.

Even the great bodhisattvas are incapable of fully explaining his life example, but in brief I will narrate it as follows.

In the dharmakaya realm of the Luminous Vajra Essence, Guru Rinpoche has by nature attained perfect enlightenment since the very beginning as the liberated ground of primordial purity. He is renowned as the original protector, Unchanging Light.

In the self-manifest sambhogakaya realm of the Thunder of the Drum of Perfection, he spontaneously manifested as the boundless wisdom array of the five families of Buddha Immense Ocean possessing the five certainties.

As the external manifestation of this self-appearing display, in the countless displays of bodily forms in buddha-fields of the five families comprised of the semimanifest natural nirmanakaya realms of Mahabrahma, he appears to all the bodhisattvas on the ten bhumis. Since these all are the cloud banks of Guru Rinpoche's wisdom display, the "inexhaustible wheel of adornment," he is known as the All-Holding Lotus.

By the power of these wisdom displays he appears in countless worlds of the ten directions as the magical apparition of nirmanakayas who tame beings. In particular, it is taught that only in this saha world system he illuminates fifty worlds with the lamp of the teachings of sutra and tantra appearing as the eight manifestations to tame beings in the different parts of the world.

The dakini Yeshe Tsogyal had a vision in which she saw a manifestation of Guru Rinpoche called Immense Vajra Ocean in the direction to the east. Each of the pores in his body held one billion realms and in each realm there were one billion world systems. In each of these world systems there were one billion Guru Rinpoches, who each created one billion emanations. Each of these emanations carried out the activity of taming one billion disciples. She then saw the same display in each of the other directions and in the center.

In this world of Jambudvipa, Guru Rinpoche is known as just one nirmanakaya who tames beings[1] but according to the different capacities and giftedness of people he is perceived in various ways. The history of *The Oral Transmission of Kilaya* and most Indian sources explain that he was born as the son of a king or a minister in Uddiyana, whereas the terma treasures for the most part narrate that he was miraculously born. In some texts he is said to have appeared from a bolt of lightning at the summit of Mount Malaya. Each of these wondrous stories differs in many ways. This is indeed a topic that lies far beyond the reach of an ordinary person's intellect.

I shall now limit the explanation down to a mere seed, the life of

---

1. A "nirmanakaya who tames beings" appears in the six realms of samsara, as opposed to an emanation in a natural nirmanakaya realm such as Buddha Amitabha's pure land Sukhavati.

Guru Rinpoche according to miraculous birth as it appears in the terma teachings.

In the land of Uddiyana situated to the west of Bodhgaya there was an island in Lake Danakosha, on which appeared a multicolored lotus flower through the blessings of the buddhas. Buddha Amitabha sent from his heart center a golden vajra marked with the letter HRIH into the bud of this lotus flower, which miraculously turned into a small child eight years of age holding a vajra and a lotus and adorned with the major and minor marks. The child remained there teaching the profound Dharma to the devas and dakinis on the island.

At that time Indrabodhi, who was the king of the country, had no sons. He had already emptied out his treasury by making offerings to the Three Jewels and giving alms to the poor. As a last resort, in order to find a wish-fulfilling jewel, he embarked on a journey on the great lake with his minister Krishnadhara. On their return, first Krishnadhara and later King Indrabodhi met the miraculous child. The king regarded him as an answer to his prayers for a son and brought him to the palace, where he was given the name Padmakara, the Lotus-Born. Padmakara was then asked to sit on a throne made of precious gems and given lavish offerings by all the people.

The prince grew up, bringing countless beings to maturation through his youthful sports and games. He married Prabhadhari and ruled the kingdom of Uddiyana in accordance with the Dharma. At that time he perceived that he would be unable to accomplish the immense welfare of other beings by governing a country, so he asked Indrabodhi permission to leave, which was not granted. In an act of play, he then pretended that his trident had slipped out of his hand; it fell and killed the son of one of the ministers. He was then sentenced to be expelled to a charnel ground. He remained in Cool Grove, Joyful Forest, and Sosaling, engaging in the conduct of yogic disciplines. During this time he received empowerment and blessings from the two dakinis Tamer of Mara and Sustainer of Bliss. When bringing all the dakinis of the charnel grounds under his command, he was known as Shantarakshita.

Padmakara returned to Uddiyana, to the island in the lake, where he practiced Secret Mantra and the symbolic language of the dakinis, through which he brought the dakinis on the island under his command. He then practiced in the Rugged Forest and was blessed with a vision of Vajra Yogini. He bound under oath all the nagas of the lakes as well as the planetary spirits and was invested with supernatural powers by all the dakas and dakinis. Thus he became renowned as Dorje Drakpo Tsal (Wrathful Vajra Power).

He then journeyed to the vajra throne in Bodhgaya, where he showed many miracles. People asked who he was, and when he replied that he was a self-appeared buddha, they did not believe him but instead defamed him. Seeing the many reasons to have a teacher, he went to Sahor, where he took ordination from Prabhahasti and was given the name Shakya Senge. He received the teaching on Yoga Tantra eighteen times and had visions of the deities. Then he went to the female master Kungamo, who was the wisdom dakini Guhya Jnana appearing in the form of a nun. He asked for empowerment, and she changed him into the letter HUNG, which she then swallowed and emitted through her lotus. Inside her body he was bestowed with the entire outer, inner, and secret empowerments and purified of the three obscurations.

Later he met the eight great vidyadharas and received the Eight Sadhana Sections. He received Maya Jala from the great master Buddha Guhya and Dzogchen from Shri Singha. In this way he studied and received all the sutras, tantras, and sciences from numerous learned and accomplished masters of India. He became adept by learning a topic just once and had visions of all the deities even without practicing. At this time he was known as Loden Choksey, and he displayed the manner of perfecting the vidyadhara level of maturation.

He then went to the country of Sahor, where he magnetized Mandarava, a qualified dakini who was the daughter of King Vihardhara. He took her as his sadhana support, and they practiced for three months in the Maratika Cave, after which Buddha Amitayus appeared in person, conferred empowerment upon them, and blessed them to be inseparable from himself. They were given one billion tantras on longevity and accomplished the vidyadhara level of life mastery. Having attained the vajra body beyond birth and death, they went back to teach the kingdom of Sahor. When begging for alms, they were arrested by the king and his ministers and burned alive. The master and his consort inspired faith by displaying the miracle of transforming the pyre into a cool lake, in the center of which they sat on a lotus flower. They caused all the people to embrace Dharma practice and established them in the state beyond falling back into samsara.

Padmakara then returned to convert the people of Uddiyana. While begging for alms, he was recognized and burned in a huge pyre of sandalwood. The master and his consort again appeared unharmed on a lotus flower in the center of a lake, wearing a garland of skulls to symbolize the liberation of all sentient beings from samsara. Because of showing this miracle he was then renowned as Padma Thotreng Tsal (Powerful Lotus of the Garland of Skulls). He remained in Uddiyana for thirteen years as the king's teacher and established the whole kingdom in Dharma practice. During this time he gave the empowerment and teachings for Kadue Chokyi Gyamtso, the Dharma Ocean Embodying All Teachings, through which the king and queen as well as all the destined ones accomplished the supreme vidyadhara level. He was then known as Padma Raja (Lotus King).

In accordance with a prophecy in the *Sutra on Magical Perception*, Padmakara transformed himself into the monk Wangpo Dey in order to convert King Ashoka. Having established Ashoka in unshakable faith, during a single night he erected in this world one million stupas containing the relics of the Tathagata. He also subdued several non-Buddhist teachers and was poisoned by one king but remained unharmed. When he then was thrown into the river, he made the river flow upstream and danced about in midair. Through that he became known as Powerful Garuda Youth.

Moreover, Padmakara manifested himself in the form of Acharya Padmavajra, the master who revealed the *Hevajra Tantra,* as well as the Brahmin Saraha, Dombi Heruka, Virupa, Kalacharya, and many other siddhas. He practiced in the great charnel grounds, where he taught the Secret Mantra to the dakinis. He subdued the outer and inner mundane spirits and named them protectors of the Dharma. At that time he became known as Nyima Oser.

When five hundred non-Buddhist teachers were about to defeat the Dharma in debate at Bodhgaya, Padmakara challenged them and was victorious. Some of the teachers resorted to evil spells, but Padmakara scattered them by means of a wrathful mantra given by the dakini Tamer of Mara. The rest converted to Buddhism, and the banner of the Dharma was raised to the skies. At that time he became known as Senge Dradrok. At this point he had exhausted the three defilements and resided on the vidyadhara level of life mastery, the stage of having fully perfected the supreme path.

Proceeding to the cave of Yanglesho, situated between India and Nepal, he met Shakya Devi, the daughter of a Nepalese king, whom he accepted as his sadhana support and consort. While he was practicing Vishuddha Heruka, three powerful spirits created obstacles, preventing rainfall for three years causing disease and famine. Padmakara sent messengers to India asking his masters for a teaching that could counteract these obstacles. Two men returned loaded with Kilaya scriptures, and the obstacles were spontaneously pacified the very moment the men arrived in Nepal. Padmakara and his consort then attained the supreme siddhi and abided on the vidyadhara level of mahamudra.

Guru Rinpoche perceived that the practice of Vishuddha Heruka brings great accomplishment. But that practice is like a traveling trader who meets with many hindrances, whereas Kilaya is like an indispensable escort. Because of this coincidence Guru Rinpoche composed many sadhanas combining the two herukas. At this place he also bound under oath the sixteen mundane protectors of Vajra Kilaya.

Padmakara visited other ancient kingdoms where he taught the Dharma: Hurmudzu in the vicinity of Uddiyana, Sikojhara, Dharmakosha, Rugma, Tirahuti, Kamarupa, and Kancha, as well as many others. It is not sure when he went to the land of Droding, but the tantric teachings he gave there on Hevajra, Guhyachandra Bindu, Vishuddha, Hayagriva, Kilaya, and Mamo are still continued in the present day.

Padmakara is generally considered to have lived in India for thirty-six hundred years benefiting the teachings and sentient beings. But it seems that learned people accept that to be half-years and simply a generalization.

In order to convert people in Mongolia and China, Padmakara emanated in the form of the King Ngonshe Chen and the yogi Tobden. Moreover, he appeared in the country of Shangshung as the miraculously born child Tavi Hricha, who gave the instructions on the hearing lineage of Dzogchen and led many worthy disciples to the attainment of the rainbow body.

In this way Padmakara's activity for bringing people to the path of liberation by means of appearing in various places, in various forms, speaking various languages, is indeed beyond measure.

Now I will describe how Padamakara came here to the land of Tibet. When King Trisong Deutsen, himself an emanation of Manjushri, was twenty years of age, he formed a strong aspiration to spread the sacred teachings of the Dharma. He invited Khenpo Bodhisattva[2] from India, who taught about dependent origination and the ten virtuous actions. A year later the foundation was laid for a huge temple, but the spirits of Tibet created obstacles and prevented the building. In accordance with the Khenpo's prediction, the king sent five runners to invite the great master Padmakara to come. Having foreknowledge of this, Padmakara had already gone to Mangyul between Nepal and Tibet. On the way to central Tibet he went via Ngari, Tsang, and Dokham and miraculously visited all of the districts, where he bound under oath the twelve Tenma goddesses, the thirteen Gurlha and twenty-one Genyen, as well as many other powerful spirits.

At the Tamarisk Forest at Red Rock he met the king of Tibet and proceeded to the top of Hepori to bring the gods and demons under his command. He laid the foundation for Samye and saw it through to completion, employing also the gods and demons who had earlier hindered the building. In five years the work was completed for the

---

2. Khenpo Bodhisattva is usually known by the name Shantarakshita, the Indian master who ordained the first monks in Tibet.

temple complex of Glorious Samye, the Unchanging and Spontaneously Accomplished Vihara, including the three temples of the queens, which was built to resemble Mount Sumeru surrounded by the four continents, eight subcontinents, sun and moon, and the wall of iron mountains. During the consecration ceremony five wondrous signs occurred.

The king then wished to translate the scriptures and establish the Dharma, so he had many intelligent Tibetan boys study to become translators. Inviting other masters of the Tripitaka from India, he had the Khenpo ordain the first seven monks and gradually establish an ordained sangha. The Khenpo Bodhisattva and Padmakara and the other panditas, together with Vairochana, Kawa Paltseg, and Chog-ro Lui Gyaltsen and the other translators, then rendered into Tibetan all the existent Buddhist scriptures on sutra and tantra as well as most of the treatises explaining them.

Vairochana and Namkhai Nyingpo were sent to India, where Vairochana studied Dzogchen with Shri Singha while Namkhai Nyingpo received the teachings on Vishuddha Heruka from the great master Hungkara. They both attained accomplishment and spread the teachings in Tibet.

King Trisong Deutsen then requested empowerment and instruction from Padmakara. At Chimphu, the hermitage above Samye, the great master disclosed the mandala of eight heruka sadhanas, into which he initiated nine chief disciples, including the king. Each of them was entrusted with a specific transmission, and all nine attained siddhi through practicing the teachings.

Padmakara gave numberless other profound and extraordinary teachings connected with the three inner tantras to many destined students headed by the king and his sons and the twenty-five disciples in Lhodrak, Tidro, and many other places.

Guru Rinpoche remained in Tibet for fifty-five years and six months, forty-eight years while the king was alive and seven years and six months afterward. He arrived when the king was twenty-one (810 C.E.). The king passed away at the age of sixty-nine. Padmakara stayed for a few years after that before leaving for the land of the rakshas.

Padmakara visited in person the twenty snow mountains of Ngari, the twenty-one places of practice in central Tibet and Tsang, the twenty-five places of Dokham, the three hidden valleys, and numerous other places, each of which he blessed to be a sacred place of practice. Knowing that a descendant of the king would later try to destroy Buddhism in Tibet, he gave many predictions for the future. Conferring with the king and the close disciples, Padmakara concealed countless terma teachings headed by the eight personal treasures of the king, the five great mind treasures, and the twenty-five profound treasures. The reasons for hiding these termas were to prevent the destruction of the teachings of Secret Mantra, to avoid the corruption of the Vajrayana or its modification by intellectuals, to preserve the blessings, and to benefit future disciples. For each of these hidden treasures Padmakara predicted the time of the disclosure, the person who would reveal it, and the destined recipients who would hold the teachings. He manifested in the terrifying wrathful form of crazy wisdom in the thirteen places named Tiger's Nest, binding all the mundane spirits under oath to serve the Dharma, and entrusted them to guard the terma treasures. At that time he was named Dorje Drollo.

To inspire faith in future generations, he left an imprint of his body at Bumthang, handprints at Namtso Chugmo, and footprints at Paro Drakar as well as in innumerable other places of practice.

After the death of King Trisong Deutsen, Padmakara placed Mutig Tsenpo on the throne. He performed a drubchen at Tramdruk, where he entrusted the profound teachings to Gyalsey Lhaje, the second prince, and gave him the prophecy that he would benefit beings by becoming a revealer of the hidden treasures in thirteen future lives.[3]

It is impossible to count exactly how many students in Tibet received empowerment from Padmakara in person, but the most renowned are the original twenty-five disciples, the intermediate twenty-five disciples, and the later seventeen and twenty-one disciples. There were eighty of his students who attended the rainbow body at

---

3. The thirteenth of these incarnations was the great treasure revealer Chokgyur Lingpa.

Yerpa and also the one hundred and eight meditators at Chuwori, the thirty tantrikas at Yangdzong, and the fifty-five realized ones at Sheldrag. Of female disciples there were the twenty-five dakini students and seven yoginis. Many of these close disciples had blood lines that have continued until the present day.

When he was about to leave for the land of rakshas to the southwest, the king, the ministers, and all the disciples tried to dissuade Padmakara from parting, but to no avail. He gave each of them extensive advice and teachings, and departed from the pass of Gungthang, riding on a horse or a lion, accompanied by numerous divine beings making offerings. At the summit of the Glorious Copper-Colored Mountain on the Chamara continent he liberated Raksha Thotreng, the king of the rakshas, and assumed his form. After that, he miraculously created the palace of Lotus Light endowed with inconceivable decorations and also emanated a replica of himself on each of the surrounding eight islands, where they reside as kings teaching the eight heruka sadhanas.

At present he dwells on the vidyadhara level of spontaneous presence in the form of the regent of Vajradhara, unshakable for as long as samsara remains. Full of compassion he sends out emanations to benefit beings. Even after the teachings of the vinaya have perished, he will appear among the tantric practitioners. There will be many destined disciples who attain the rainbow body. In the future, when Buddha Maitreya appears in this world, Padmakara will emanate as the one known as Drowa Kundul and spread the teachings of Secret Mantra to all worthy people.

This short biography is just a partial narration that conforms to what was perceived by some ordinary students.[4]

---

4. Jamgon Kontrul was himself a reincarnation of the translator Vairocana. He had many visions of Guru Rinpoche and was also a revealer of terma teachings.

Introductory Teaching

In the world period that we are now in, one thousand buddhas will appear. In the same way, for each of these buddhas there will be one thousand Guru Rinpoches to carry out their activities. In the present age of Buddha Shakyamuni one such emanation appeared in the person of Padmasambhava, the Lotus-Born One. It is said in Padmasambhava's life story that he was spontaneously born without a father or mother from a lotus flower in a lake. As a miraculously born human being, he was endowed with great powers capable of subduing not only human beings but also spirits and other different types of nonhumans. He lived for quite a long time. He stayed in India for roughly a thousand years and then spent fifty-five years in Tibet. When about to leave Tibet, he was accompanied by his twenty-five chief disciples and the king. At the border of Nepal he was escorted by dakinis of the four classes on a horse called Mahabala. This fabulous horse flew into the skies, leaving the disciples to watch Guru Rinpoche's image slowly disappear, becoming smaller and smaller.

According to the story, Padmasambhava descended to Bodhgaya and stayed there for some time. He then went on to his pure land, which is known as Sangdok Palri, the Glorious Copper-Colored Mountain. Physically it is a large island, a kind of subcontinent, situated in the ocean to the southwest of Bodhgaya. The island has several levels. The lower levels are inhabited by rakshas. According to the predictions of Buddha Shakyamuni, these cannibal spirits would invade the known world in a later historical period when the average life span of human beings would approach twenty years. Posing a great danger, the rakshas would subdue and destroy all human beings. The Buddha also predicted that Guru Rinpoche should go to their continent and conquer these rakshas. Guru Rinpoche fulfilled that prediction.

The main mountain on this copper-colored island descends deep below the ocean into the naga realm. At the peak the summit pierces the skies even to the level of the Brahma world in the realm of form. On the very tip of this mountain there is a miraculously manifested buddha realm with three levels. Uppermost is the dharmakaya emanation of Guru Rinpoche, as Buddha Amitayus; in the middle level is Guru Rinpoche's sambhogakaya form, Avalokiteshvara, and on the ground level is the nirmanakaya form, Guru Rinpoche himself, surrounded by the eight manifestations. Guru Rinpoche is the mind emanation of Amitabha, the speech emanation of Avalokiteshvara, and the body emanation of the Buddha Shakyamuni. Before manifesting in this world, he appeared first in the sambhogakaya realm as the five families of Thotreng Tsal, then as the eight and twelve manifestations, and finally in countless emanations.

Before leaving Tibet, Guru Rinpoche made many predictions and hid many teachings that were to be revealed in the future. He blessed his close disciples so that they would be inseparable from himself. In future reincarnations they would reveal the hidden teachings. Endowed with great miraculous powers like Guru Rinpoche himself, they were able to fly through the sky, traverse freely through solid matter, and also be unimpeded in expounding the sutras and the treatises, as well as the meaning of the tantras. In particular Guru Rinpoche prophesied the coming of 108 great tertons, revealers of hidden treasures. Because of changes and fluctuations in world history, each terton would appear in designated times to benefit beings facing difficulties. Being aware of future problems, Guru Rinpoche concealed specific practices especially suited to the time in which they were to be revealed. The tertons discovering them would then have a teaching that was totally fresh, up to date, and meant for that specific time and situation. For example, just as we prefer to have fresh food prepared in a way that will not make us sick, in the same way the terma teachings are endowed with very special qualities. One quality is that termas have a short lineage that has not been interrupted by any breaking or damage of samaya; also, the termas have not been interpolated by others. Hidden teachings come directly from Guru Rinpoche and are revealed by his disciples in future incarnations; then they are spread among people for immediate practice.

To reiterate and expand in short, the special quality of the terma teachings concealed by Guru Rinpoche is that they provide a method for accomplishment appropriate for each generation, period of time, and individual person who meets them. Every terton reveals fresh teachings that are to be practiced by destined people. Older termas may have been flawed by broken samayas, delaying the signs of attainment. Therefore, for quick accomplishment, the new termas have greater blessings. Furthermore, most people, including Tibetans, have some fondness for novelty. New termas seem more interesting! Tibetans have slightly less faith in older termas, and the result of practice is somehow delayed. The greater faith and trust in fresh, flawless termas causes greater industry in practice and, consequently, swifter results. These are the factors for the coincidence of new termas appearing. Otherwise, one terma for each of the Three Roots of guru, yidam, and dakini would be sufficient. But people are so fond of novelties; a new terton with a new revelation of terma teachings causes tremendous joy and amazement. That is one of the skillful means of Guru Rinpoche, which itself is truly amazing.

Yeshe Tsogyal was one of five dakini emanations of Vajra Yogini and, in essence, also a manifestation of Guru Rinpoche himself. She appeared to assist Guru Rinpoche in spreading the Vajrayana, especially the terma teachings, in the snowy land of Tibet.

Externally, the word *dakini* literally means "sky-dweller," a celestial being who does not need to walk on the ground. There are different types of dakinis: wisdom dakinis, activity dakinis, and mundane dakinis. The real wisdom dakini is the empty quality of luminous wakefulness. Perception is the male aspect, while emptiness within our perception is the female quality. Thus the great mother of dharmakaya is the basis for all the dakinis.

Actually, the basis for all male deities is the dharmakaya buddha Samantabhadra and the basis for all female deities is Samantabhadri. Samantabhadra is the foundation of all perception and Samantabhadri is the empty quality within all these perceptions. Moreover, while Samantabhadri is called the ground of emanation, her emanation is the great mother of dharmakaya, the female buddha Prajnaparamita. Vajra Varahi is a sambhogakaya emanation of Prajnaparamita, as are the five female buddhas Dhatvishvari, Mamaki, Buddhalochana, Pandaravasini, and Samayatara, who are consorts of the five male buddhas. On the nirmanakaya level Prajnaparamita's emanation is Arya Tara. These were the wisdom dakinis of the three kayas.

In addition to wisdom dakinis, there are also the dakinis who carry out the activities of enlightened deeds for the welfare of beings, the samaya dakinis who oversee the observation of our tantric commitments, samayas. There are also the dakinis who live in the major and minor sacred places in this world: the thirty-two major sacred areas and the twenty-four minor sacred valleys. When including the eight chief charnel grounds, these are renowned as the sixty-four sacred places where the sixty-four dakas and dakinis dwell. Corresponding to these sixty-four external places, on a more subtle level, the same number of dakas and dakinis also dwell in sixty-four centers of our physical body as the pure essence of the channels, energies, and essences.

Yeshe Tsogyal was also an emanation of Arya Tara. Arya Tara is an emanation of Vajra Varahi. Vajra Varahi's ground of emanation is Prajnaparamita and Samantabhadri. The equivalent male three kayas are Samantabhadra, Vajradhara, and Buddha Shakyamuni. It is quite foolish to say that only men and not women become buddhas since both Prajnaparamita and Samantabhadri are buddhas. The five aspects of Vajra Varahi are also fully enlightened buddhas. Arya Tara appears in the form of a bodhisattva on the tenth bhumi but in actuality she is also a completely awakened buddha. Moreover, the eight female bodhisattvas among the forty-two peaceful deities are also buddhas. The attribute of being male or female is definitely not ultimate. The eight male and female bodhisattvas among the peaceful deities in the bardo state are identical in essence with the eight mamo goddesses and eight yoginis, all female, among the wrathful deities. Male buddhas appear as female and female as male. Dakinis can appear in all different ways and forms, some of them outrageous or repulsive in order to arrest conceptual thinking and wrong perception.

Finally, when practicing the Dharma it is good to remember that the special quality of the Vajrayana system of the early translations and, especially, of the teachings of Dzogchen is "to ascend with the conduct while descending with the view." This statement of Guru Rinpoche is of crucial importance. If we start out by acting according to a high view, we will simply look crazy or insane. If we only keep the view of the lower vehicles we will never find the chance for liberation. The view of a shravaka or pratyekabuddha does not bring enlightenment in one lifetime but only after three incalculable aeons. One must act in accordance with the lower vehicles while keeping the view of the inner tantras.

TULKU URGYEN RINPOCHE
Asura Cave, 1989

Dakini Teachings

First of All
The Teachings of Ascending with the Conduct

The Master Padmakara appeared in different forms with various kinds of attire. In the manner that is beyond observance he observed all the precepts, ranging from the disciplines of the shravakas to the tantric vows of the vidyadharas. He orally taught the nine gradual vehicles and thus showed the view and conduct as a unity, descending with the view while ascending with the conduct. Since his mind possessed the realization of total omniscience, he cherished with bodhicitta all sentient beings higher than himself.

All the advice on how to behave spoken by this master, who was a nirmanakaya in person, an enlightened one, was written down by Lady Tsogyal.

The great master said: Whichever teaching of the outer or inner vehicles you practice, you must first take refuge in the Three Jewels. While possessing the precepts that are the foundation of your training,[1] whenever you go in a certain direction, take refuge in the buddhas and bodhisattvas of that direction.

Always have unwavering faith in the Three Jewels. By so doing, you create a karmic connection right now, and in the future you will become the disciple of the buddhas. It is therefore essential to make offerings and supplications to the Three Jewels.

Master Padma said: Practice the Dharma of the ten virtuous actions and have confidence in what should be avoided and what should be

---

1. The particular set of vows one has taken of any of the three vehicles.

undertaken concerning the "black and white" types of the effects of these actions. By doing so your actions will hold great strength.

Since the power of truth is great, give up all nonvirtue and misdeeds, apply the remedy that works against your disturbing emotions, and put great effort into meritorious actions.

One who has not gathered merit will not engender a noble attitude. One who accumulates merit will have a noble frame of mind. Once you hold the noble attitude in your being, you will put effort into virtue and refrain from misdeeds. It is therefore essential to arouse diligence in the different types of means for gathering merit through your body, speech, and mind.

Master Padma said: To arouse bodhicitta, the mind set upon supreme enlightenment, before undertaking any Dharma practice, is most important. The person who has aroused bodhicitta will cultivate the feeling of equality that all beings are his mothers, free from partiality and prejudice, in order to serve all sentient beings.

Of all sentient beings there is not a single one who has not been your own father or mother. So as a way of repaying the kindness of all sentient beings, set out to work for their well-being.

Cultivate loving-kindness and compassion for all sentient beings. Constantly train yourself in bodhicitta. Train yourself to benefit sentient beings through all your actions. Train yourself in cherishing others as more important than yourself.

In short, the most essential point is that the determination of arousing bodhicitta must precede all the outer and inner practices and the stages of development and completion.

Generation of bodhicitta is the very root of all Dharma practice.

Master Padma said: If you desire to attain the buddhahood of omniscience then train yourself in understanding that all ego clinging and fixation on phenomena have no self-nature.

No matter what meritorious action you may be involved in, understand that all phenomena are like dreams and magic.

In accordance with my oral instruction, train yourself in the emptiness of all phenomena without clinging either to the six paramitas or to great compassion.

By the power of meditating on emptiness you should come to realize that the six paramitas and the engendered great compassion are also like a magical illusion.

Although you meditate on emptiness, make sure that it becomes an aid to virtuous practice and a remedy against your disturbing emotions.

Whatever root of virtue you engage in, fuel it with bodhicitta and never be separate from the six paramitas.

Whatever you then do, always have the intention to increase virtue and decrease misdeeds.

Whatever physical actions you engage in, make them virtuous. Whatever words you utter, make them virtuous. Whatever thoughts you entertain, make them virtuous.

In short, exert yourself in nothing but wholesome and virtuous actions of body, speech, and mind. Shun even the tiniest nonvirtue or misdeed.

If you do not keep the protection of the armor of mindfulness and conscientiousness, the weapons of disturbing emotions will cut the aorta for attaining the higher realms and liberation. During the four kinds of daily activities, it is therefore essential to guard yourself with the armor of mindfulness and conscientiousness.

Master Padma said: First of all, have confidence in the cause and effect of your actions.

Keep in mind that before long you will definitely die. This life lasts only for a short while so do not strive for the things of this life.

Keep in mind the future is lasting and strive for the benefit of the future.

Make ready and certain now, for the benefit of future lives, that you do not slip onto a downward track.

Do not be conceited about anything. If you retain the pride of thinking that you are learned, great, or noble, you will not acquire any good qualities. So cast away conceit and train yourself in Dharma practice without wavering for even a single moment.

Apply the remedies against misdeeds. If even the slightest disturbing emotion or unvirtuous deed arises in your being, think of it as an unbearable suffering, the size of Mount Sumeru.

Actions engaged in with doubt will not accomplish anything, so do not harbor the slightest doubt.

As long as you have not abandoned ego-clinging, then misdeeds, no matter how small, will still yield results. So it is essential to shun misdeeds.

Master Padma said: Having taken the vows of the greater or lesser vehicles,[2] do not abandon them even at the cost of your life. If you do damage them, it is most important to immediately make confession and retake your vows.

Some people, when their vows are damaged, become disheartened and commit nothing but acts of further transgression. But like cleansing oneself by washing and sprinkling fragrant water after slipping in the dirt, purify your obscurations and acts of downfall and violation so that broken vows never accumulate.

Do not keep company with or befriend a person who has degenerated his discipline or samayas for even a single moment. If when wearing white robes you go to an oily swamp, the black stuff will surely discolor the white. Similarly, even though your own samayas are pure you will surely still be defiled by the broken samayas of others. If your own samayas are not pure, it is like black not being tainted by black. So be very careful.

It is there essential not to associate with evil people or with bad company who have lost their vows.

In any case, one should take care not to be ashamed of oneself.

Master Padma said: Whatever actions you engage in, do not do anything nondharmic that fails to become the accumulation of merit and wisdom.

---

2. The bodhisattva vow and the refuge precepts. The latter also includes the vows of individual liberation. See the glossary.

Do not desire anything other than omniscient buddhahood and benefiting sentient beings.

Do not be attached to anything. Attachment itself is the root of bondage.

Do not criticize other teachings and do not disparage people. All the teachings are ultimately indivisible, like the taste of salt.

Do not criticize any of the higher or lower vehicles. They are identical in being the path to be journeyed, just like the steps on a staircase.

You cannot know another person unless you can perceive with superknowledge. So do not criticize others.

In general, all sentient beings are by their very nature spontaneously perfect buddhas. They possess the essence of enlightenment. Do not examine other people's faults or delusions.

Do not examine the limitations of others. Examine how you can change your own.

Do not examine the shortcomings of others but examine your own shortcomings.

The greatest of evils is to hold religious prejudice and to criticize other people without knowing their mind. So give up prejudice as if it were poison.

Master Padma said: Even though you have taken so many rebirths since beginningless time, you have not accomplished the welfare of yourself and others. Now, in this body, you should accomplish the benefit of self and others.

Even though you have incarnated so many times in the past, you had no opportunity to train in the Dharma but only plunged further into the dungeon of samsaric existence. Now exert yourself in training in the Mahayana teachings during this brief time while you have met the Dharma.

Keep company with those who increase virtue. Give up friends who increase misdeeds.

Do not restlessly hanker after things like a dog or a hungry ghost, but rest loosely by means of applying the remedies. If you tire yourself with restless hankering, you will agitate your own mind with evil deeds, and through that the minds of others. Thus you will accumulate misdeeds.

If you consider even slight discomfort to be suffering, it will grow to be more painful. You will find no happiness unless you let your mind rest loosely.

Do not pursue former suffering. Everything, whether good or bad, is past and gone. Do not anticipate future suffering.

No matter what suffering may befall you now, do not give in to it, but develop courage again and again.

In any case, if you do not apply the remedies to your mind, suffering will never cease.

Relax your mind in its natural state without modifying or spoiling it and turn it gently to what is virtuous.

Master Padma said: When you persevere in Dharma practice, it is essential to always train in turning any virtuous root of action, through body, speech, or mind, to be for the benefit of others.

First, train gradually in this with the smallest deeds. From time to time, check to see whether or not you are tainted by the defilement of self-interest. You will not be successful if you retain even the tiniest taint of selfishness. Make sure not to be tainted by the defilement of self-interest.

The difference between the greater and lesser vehicles is the arousing of bodhicitta. The difference is created not by the view but by compassion. Therefore keeping the view of the natural state, train yourself in great compassion.

For the benefit of self and others, abandon the suffering of samsara forever.

Train repeatedly in feeling renunciation for samsara.

Train in taking upon yourself the burden of the suffering of others.

First train in regarding all sentient beings as being like yourself. Train in feeling that the suffering of others is your own suffering. Then train in cherishing sentient beings as being more important than yourself.

Train in the great compassion that involuntarily acts for the welfare of others.

The word *Mahayana* implies simply to cherish others as being superior to oneself. Mahayana never implies the pursuit of happiness solely for oneself with no thought for the suffering of others, regarding oneself as more important.

Master Padma said: If you train your mind in love, compassion, and bodhicitta, you will not take rebirth in the three lower realms. Moreover, from this very moment you will never fall back. This alone is my oral instruction.

Wherever you go, keep bodhicitta in mind, never departing from its company.

Whatever action you engage in, train in doing it for the benefit of sentient beings. Train in regarding others as more important than yourself. You will attain numerous qualities as a result of this training, such as having unimpaired samayas and vows.

Unless you cultivate bodhicitta, you will not attain enlightenment, even though you may gain mastery of mantra and be very powerful.

All the supreme and common accomplishments will result from bodhicitta arising in your being. That alone is my oral instruction.

Master Padma said: Whether you meditate on emptiness or anything else, it is mistaken meditation practice unless it becomes an effective remedy against disturbing emotions and ordinariness. Something that does not counteract the disturbing emotions and ordinariness is a cause for falling into samsaric existence.

If any teaching you study, reflect upon, or expound becomes an effective remedy against your disturbing emotions as well as an aid for allowing the pure Dharma to take birth in your being, then that is called a Mahayana teaching and is unmistaken.

No matter how much you may be acclaimed as learned in study, exposition, and meditation, if your intention is only the eight worldly concerns, your activity is called a black Dharma practice.

In any case, it is essential to meditate on appearance and existence[3]

---

3. "Appearance and existence" refers to the universe with all sentient beings.

as being magical illusion, so as not to allow your attachment and clinging to grow stronger and stronger.

"A great yogi" simply means being free from attachment and clinging.

Master Padma said: The welfare and happiness of all sentient beings result from the teachings of the Buddha. So study the tantras, scriptures, and sutras and listen to the words of the masters.

Actions and their resulting happiness and suffering grow forth like seeds, so discriminate between virtue and evil deeds.

If you do not observe your vows, the root of your Dharma practice is rotten. Protect your vows and samayas as carefully as you would your own eyes.

In any case, if you have no trust when practicing the Dharma your effort is wasted, and anything you do will be futile. In whatever you do it is essential to be free from doubt and mistrust.

Master Padma said: Some people call themselves tantric practitioners and engage in crude behavior, but that is not the action of a tantrika.

Mahayana means to cherish all sentient beings with impartial compassion.

It will not suffice to claim oneself a tantric practitioner and then refrain from adopting what is virtuous and not avoiding or shunning evil deeds. It is essential for all tantric practitioners to cultivate great compassion in their being.

Without giving rise to compassion in your being you will turn into a non-Buddhist with wrong views, even though you may claim to be a practitioner of Secret Mantra.

Master Padma said: Secret Mantra is Mahayana. *Mahayana* means to benefit others.

In order to benefit others you must attain the three kayas of fruition. In order to attain the three kayas you must gather the two accumulations. In order to gather the two accumulations you must train in bodhicitta. You must practice the paths of development and completion as a unity.

In any case, a tantrika who lacks bodhicitta is totally unsuited and does not practice Mahayana.

Master Padma said: Secret Mantra and the philosophical vehicle[4] are spoken of as two, but ultimately they are one. If you lack the view or the conduct you will stray into being a shravaka. So descend with the view while ascending with the conduct. It is most essential to practice these two as a unity. That is my oral instruction.

SAMAYA.

This completes the teaching on ascending with the conduct.

This was committed to writing at the upper hermitage of Chimphu on the eighth day of the last summer month in the Year of the Hare.

Seal of treasure.
Seal of concealment.
Seal of entrustment.

---

4. Another word for the Mahayana teachings or the paramita vehicle.

Taking Refuge

The Master Padmakara of Uddiyana, who appeared as a nirmanakaya in person, was asked by Lady Tsogyal, the princess of Kharchen: Great Master, please be kind and teach the basis for all Dharma practice, the means by which to end birth and death, a little cause that has immense benefit, a method that is easy to apply and has little hardship.

The nirmanakaya master replied: Tsogyal, taking refuge is the basis for all Dharma practice. The Three Jewels are the support for all Dharma practice. The means that brings an end to birth and death is to take refuge along with its subsidiary aspects.

Lady Tsogyal asked: What is the essential meaning of taking refuge? What is its definition? When divided, how many types are there?

The master replied: The essential meaning of taking refuge is to accept the Buddha, Dharma, and Sangha as your teacher, path, and companions for practicing the path, and then to pledge that they are the fruition you will attain. Thus taking refuge means a pledge or acceptance. Why is such an acceptance called taking refuge? It is called taking refuge because of accepting the Buddha, Dharma, and Sangha as the support, refuge, and protector or rescuer for being freed from the great fear of the sufferings and obscurations. That is the essential meaning of taking refuge.

The definition of taking refuge is to seek protection from the terrors of the three lower realms and from the inferior view of believing in a self within the transitory collection[1] as is held by non-Buddhist philosophers.

---

1. "The transitory collection" refers to the continuity of the five aggregates.

When divided, there are the three types: the outer way of taking refuge, the inner way of taking refuge, and the secret way of taking refuge.

THE OUTER WAY OF TAKING REFUGE

Lady Tsogyal asked: Concerning the outer way of taking refuge, what is the cause of wanting to take refuge? In what object does one take refuge? What kind of person takes refuge? What are the manners or methods though which one takes refuge? With what particular attitude does one take refuge?

Master Padma replied: The cause of wanting to take refuge is fear of the miseries of samsara, trusting in the Three Jewels as the place of refuge, and, moreover, accepting the Three Jewels to be the objects of refuge and the protectors of refuge. Through these three you give rise to the intention of taking refuge. In general, one wants to take refuge due to fear of death.

There are many people who do not even notice that half of their life has passed and who do not think of their future lives for even an instant. They have no refuge.

If you were not going to die or if you were certain of a human rebirth, you would not need to take refuge. However, after dying and transmigrating, there are the overwhelming miseries of the lower realms.

In what object does one take refuge? You should take refuge in the Three Jewels. Who can bring an end to birth and death? It is exclusively the omniscient Buddha who is free from all defects and who has perfected all virtues. Therefore, only the Dharma he has taught and the sangha who uphold his doctrine are able to bring an end to the cycle of birth and death of self and others. Since these are the sole objects of refuge, you should take refuge in them.

In general, there are many people who consider the teachings of the truly and perfectly enlightened one as no more than the words of a fortuneteller, and who, when pressed, go to spirits for refuge. It is difficult for such people to have refuge.

What kind of person takes refuge? The one who possesses interest,

devotion, and faith, and who thinks of the virtues of the Three Jewels.
One should possess these three particular attitudes:

> Since samsara is without beginning and end, I must turn away
>   from it this very moment!
> The gods of the non-Buddhists and so forth are not my objects
>   of refuge!
> The omniscient state of buddhahood alone is my true object of
>   refuge!

This is how the special taking refuge takes place.

When taking refuge, mere lip service is useless. This is like empty
muttering. It is uncertain where it will lead you.

What is the manner in which one takes refuge? You should take
refuge with respectful body, speech, and mind. You should take
refuge with three thoughts: fear of the lower realms and samsara,
trust in the blessings of the Three Jewels, and steadfast faith and
compassion.

The person who believes that this life is perfect and that the next
one will also be perfect will simply die while still about to practice
the Dharma. That is not enough.

In this context, you should know the rituals of taking refuge.

With what particular attitude does one take refuge? You should
take refuge with a sense of responsibility for the welfare of others.
You should take refuge with this attitude, as you will not attain the
true and complete enlightenment simply by renouncing samsara and
desiring the result of nirvana.

> In order to free all sentient beings from the miseries of samsara,
> I will take refuge until I and all the sentient beings of the three
> realms have achieved supreme enlightenment!

In general, all wishing is dualistic wishing. Taking refuge without
being free from dualistic fixation is not sufficient.

Lady Tsogyal then asked the master: How many kinds of training
does the outer way of taking refuge entail?

The master replied: As soon as you have taken refuge you must skillfully practice the eight trainings, in order to prevent your commitment from degenerating.

She asked: What are these eight trainings?

He replied: First, there are the three special trainings: Having taken refuge in the Buddha, you should not bow down to other gods; having taken refuge in the Dharma, you should give up causing harm to sentient beings; having taken refuge in the Sangha, you should not associate with heretical people. These are the three special trainings.

To explain that further: First, having taken refuge in the Buddha, "not to bow down to other gods" means that if you bow down to mundane gods such as Mahadeva, Vishnu, Maheshvara, or others, your refuge vow is damaged. If you go to such gods for refuge, your refuge vow is destroyed.

Secondly, having taken refuge in the Dharma, "to give up causing harm to sentient beings" means that your refuge vow is definitely destroyed if you engage in killing. It is damaged even if you just beat other beings out of anger, enslave them, make holes in their noses, imprison them in a cattle shack, pluck out their hair, take their wool, and so forth.

Thirdly, having taken refuge in the Sangha, "to refrain from associating with heretical people" means that your vow is damaged if you keep company with people who hold the view and conduct of eternalism or nihilism. If your view and conduct are in conformity with theirs, your refuge vow is destroyed.

In any case, all Dharma practice is included within taking refuge. People with wrong views do not have this understanding.

These are the five general trainings.

1. When beginning your practice, make an extensive offering with a vast amount of the best kinds of food and drink. Present the offerings before the Precious Ones on the fourteenth day and beseech them to arrive for the offering. Following that, make offerings on the fifteenth day. These offerings are of four kinds: the offering of prostrations, the offering of material objects, the offering of praise, and the offering of practice.

First, the offering of prostration: Stand up straight and join your palms. Thinking of the virtues of the buddhas and bodhisattvas, imagine that you are touching their feet adorned with the design of the wheel as you make prostrations.

Next is the offering of material objects: Present offerings such as flowers that are entirely unowned by anyone and visualized offerings, as well as your own body.

Make praises with melodious tunes.

The offering of practice is to make the aspiration that the roots or your virtue resulting from having cultivated the bodhicitta of undivided emptiness and compassion may be for the attainment of enlightenment for the sake of all sentient beings.

Master Padma said: The Three Precious Ones have not even an atom of need for a bowl of water or respect. The purpose of making the offering is to enable you to receive the light rays of the buddhas.

Concerning the offering of the best kinds of food and drink, make three heaps of the best type of food, and utter OM AH HUNG three times. Imagine that your offerings thereby become an ocean of nectar. Following that, envision your yidam deity surrounded by an infinite gathering of the Three Precious Ones and imagine that you present this nectar offering, requesting them all to accept it. If you are unable to offer in that way, simply make an offering while saying, "Precious Ones, accept this!"

If you do not have anything to offer, you should at least present bowls of water every day. If you do not do that, your refuge vow will degenerate.

The Precious Ones do not need these offering of material nourishment in the same way as sentient beings. The food torma is for you to gather the accumulations without noticing.

2. The second training is to not abandon the sublime Precious Ones even for the sake of your body, your life, or a valuable gift.

Regarding not abandoning the refuge even for the sake of your body: Even if someone threatens to cut your eyes out, cut off your legs, your ears, your nose, or your arms, you should let him do so rather than abandon the Precious Ones.

Regarding not abandoning the refuge even at the cost of your life:

even if someone threatens to kill you, you should let him do so rather than abandon the Precious Ones.

Regarding not abandoning the refuge for the sake of a valuable gift: even if you are promised the whole world filled with precious stones in return for giving up the refuge, you should not renounce the refuge.

3. The third training is that no matter what happens to you, whether you are sick, under hardship, at ease, happy, or sad, you should lay out a mandala and the five kinds of offerings and offer them to the Three Jewels. Then take refuge and make this supplication:

> Sacred master, great vajra holder, all buddhas and bodhisattvas, please listen to me! May all my sickness and whatever is caused by spirits and negative forces not occur. Please create peace, auspiciousness, and goodness.

Aside from this it is also appropriate to gather merit by reading the scriptures aloud, chanting, and offering tormas, since such practices belong to the basics for taking refuge. If nothing helps, do not give rise to wrong views, thinking, The Precious Ones have no blessings! The Dharma is untrue! Think instead, I shall feel better when my evil karma has become exhausted! Without pursuing other ways such as soothsaying and shamanistic rituals, engage only in taking refuge.

4. In whichever direction you travel, remember the buddhas and bodhisattvas, make offerings, and take refuge. For instance, if tomorrow you are going toward the east, lay out a mandala and make offerings today, taking refuge in the buddhas and bodhisattvas of that direction.

Which supplication should you make? You should supplicate as follows before taking leave:

> Master, vajra holder, all buddhas and bodhisattvas, please listen to me! Please prevent obstacles caused by humans and nonhumans and make everything auspicious from the time of leaving this place until I arrive at my destination.

If you do not do that the day before departure you should do it at the time of departure.

At the time of leaving, if you do not remember to take refuge within ten or seven steps of crossing your threshold, your refuge vow is damaged.

Once you entrust your mind to the refuge, it is impossible that you will be deceived.

5. Think of the good qualities of taking refuge and train in it again and again. Having taken refuge in the Three Precious Ones, regard them as your place of hope and look up to them as your place of trust. Keep the Precious Ones as your only source of refuge and make supplications to them. Pray to the Precious Ones for blessings.

Think that your present representation of the Three Jewels, whether a cast image, carved relief, a painting, a stupa, a volume of a book, or so forth, is the dharmakaya. It is possible that the essence of dharmakaya will be suddenly realized when making prostrations, offerings, or supplications. Even if that does not happen, by prostrating and making offering to the Three Jewels and creating a karmic connection, one will become a disciple of a buddha in the future.

Master Padma said: No matter what arises in you such as the virtues and happiness of the enlightened ones, regard these to be the blessings of your master and the Precious Ones. By thinking in that way, you will receive the blessings. No matter what problems and misery you may meet, regard them as your own evil karma. That will bring an end to all your negative karmas. In general, if you do not entrust your mind to the Precious Ones, but hold the wrong view of thinking, The Precious Ones have no blessings!, it is possible that you will not escape from the lowest hells.

Lady Tsogyal asked the master: What good qualities result from taking refuge?

The master replied: Taking refuge has eight good qualities.

1. You enter the group of Buddhists. Having taken refuge in the Three Jewels, you are called a Buddhist. Without having taken refuge, you are not included among the Buddhist group, even though you

may claim to be a holy person, a great meditator, or the Buddha in person.

2. You become a suitable vessel for all the vows such as the Individual Liberation. Correspondingly, if you lose your refuge vow, it is said that all the vows based thereon are also destroyed.

In order to restore them, restoring the refuge vow will be sufficient. That is to say, it is sufficient that you make an offering to the Three Jewels and take the vow in their presence.

You also need to have taken refuge prior to any vow; from the one-day precepts and so forth up to the vows of Secret Mantra. Taking refuge is therefore known as that which causes you to become a suitable basis for all types of vows.

3. The vow of taking refuge in the Three Jewels diminishes and brings to an end all karmic obscurations accumulated throughout all your past lives. That is to say, your obscurations will be totally exhausted through the special taking refuge, while through the general taking refuge the karmic obscurations will diminish.

Again, when a genuine feeling of taking refuge has arisen in your being, karmic obscurations are utterly brought to an end, while by the mere words of taking refuge they will diminish.

Furthermore, if you take refuge at all times, while walking, moving about, lying down, and sitting, the karmic obscurations will be completely exhausted, while by just taking refuge from time to time they will diminish.

4. You will possess vast merit. The mundane merits of long life, good health, splendor, and majestic dignity, great wealth and so forth, result from taking refuge. The supramundane unexcelled enlightenment also results from taking refuge.

5. You will be immune to attack by humans and nonhumans, and immune to the obstacles of this life. It is said that as soon as the genuine taking refuge has arisen in your being, you cannot be harmed by human obstacles in this life. Also you cannot be harmed by nonhumans such as nagas and malicious spirits.

6. You will achieve the fulfillment of whatever you may wish for. When the genuine taking refuge has arisen in your being, it is impossible not to accomplish whatever you intend. In short, it is said

that placing your trust in the objects of refuge, you will receive whatever you desire, just as when supplicating a wish-fulfilling gem.

7. You will not fall into the lower realms, evil destinies, or perverted paths. The "three lower realms" refers to the hells, hungry ghost, and animal realms. "Evil destinies" refers to being reborn in places devoid of the Dharma such as among primitive border tribes. "Perverted paths" refers to non-Buddhist philosophies. So in order to avoid falling into these, it is said that one should simply take refuge.

8. The final benefit is that of swiftly attaining the true and complete enlightenment. What need is there to mention other benefits!

It is said in the Mahayana teachings of Secret Mantra that one can attain enlightenment within this single body and lifetime. This means that without a doubt you will swiftly attain enlightenment. So it is necessary to cut the misconception of thinking that it is enough to take refuge just once in a while. You should take refuge again and again both day and night. Then you will definitely swiftly attain true and complete enlightenment.

Master Padma said: If you exert yourself in taking refuge, you do not need to practice many other teachings. There is no doubt that you will attain the fruition of enlightenment.

Lady Tsogyal again asked the master: What is the actual practice of taking refuge?

The master replied: The actual application of taking refuge is as follows. First, form the aspiration of thinking:

> I will establish all sentient beings in complete enlightenment. In order to do that I will gather the accumulations, purify the obscurations, and clear away the hindrances. For this purpose I will take refuge from this very moment until reaching enlightenment!

Then, without being distracted, say three times:

> In the supreme of all humans, all the buddhas of the ten directions, I and all the infinite sentient beings take refuge from this very moment until reaching supreme enlightenment.

In the supreme of all peace, devoid of attachment, the Dharma teachings of the ten directions, I and all the infinite sentient beings take refuge from this very moment until reaching supreme enlightenment.

In the supreme of all assemblies, the members of the noble sangha who are beyond falling back and who dwell in the ten directions, I and all infinite sentient beings take refuge from this very moment until reaching supreme enlightenment.

Following that, repeat many times without being distracted:

> I take refuge in the Buddha.
> I take refuge in the Dharma.
> I take refuge in the Sangha.

Then make this supplication three times:

Three Precious Ones, please protect me from the fears of this life. Please protect me from the fears of the lower realms. Please protect me from entering perverted paths!

When you are about to finish, say:

Through this, my roots of virtue, may I attain buddhahood in order to benefit beings!

You should make the dedication in this way.

Lady Tsogyal asked the nirmanakaya master Padmakara: What is the method of taking the refuge vow?

The master replied: One should prostrate to and circumambulate a master who possesses the refuge vow, present him with flowers, and say as follows.

Master, please listen to me. Buddhas and bodhisattvas in the ten directions, please listen to me. From this very moment until attaining supreme enlightenment, I, _____,² take refuge in the supreme of all humans, the billion truly perfected dharmakaya buddhas.

---

2. Say your ordinary name at this point.

I take refuge in the supreme of all peace, devoid of attachment, the teachings of Mahayana.

I take refuge in the supreme of all assemblies, the sangha of noble bodhisattvas who are beyond falling back.

At the third repetition of this you will have obtained the vow. Make prostrations and scatter flowers. Then practice the trainings explained above and exert yourself in taking refuge.

This was the explanation of the outer way of taking refuge along with its application.

Lady Tsogyal asked the master: How is one protected by having taken refuge?

The master replied: Whoever practices the trainings correctly, having taken refuge as explained above, will definitely be protected by the Three Jewels. Since this is so, if you fear straying into an errant path and pray to meet a genuine path, you will surely meet it. You will definitely also be protected from the fears of this life.

When all the qualities of taking refuge have arisen in your being, you should not be content to stop. Increase more and more the qualities that have arisen within you. You should use all the qualities that arise in your mind to gather the accumulations and purify the obscurations. When such exertion is generated, the full measure of ability has been produced.

All people who do not feel inclined to give rise to profound qualities such as [insight into] emptiness or the mandala of deities within their being can still purify their obscurations and gather the accumulations simply by taking refuge.

You may then argue, If one is protected by taking refuge in such a way, does that mean that the buddhas appear and lead all sentient beings? The reply is that the buddhas cannot take all sentient beings out of samsara with their hands. If they were able to do that, the buddhas with their great compassion and skillful means would have already freed all beings without a single exception.

Well then, you may ask, by what is one protected? The answer is that one is protected by the [practice of the] Dharma.

When taking refuge has arisen within your being, you do not need to practice other teachings. It is impossible that you will not be protected by the compassion of the Three Jewels. It is similar to the fact that you will definitely be fearless when you have an excellent escort.

Thus Master Padma explained the outer way of taking refuge to Lady Tsogyal.

THE INNER WAY OF TAKING REFUGE

The nirmanakaya master Padmakara was asked by Lady Tsogyal, the princess of Kharchen: To which inner objects does one take refuge? What kind of person takes refuge? Through which manner or method does one take refuge? Which particular attitude and what duration of time does it entail? What particular circumstance is required? What is the purpose and what are the qualities?

The master replied: Regarding the objects of refuge, you should take refuge in the guru, yidam, and dakini.

The person who takes refuge should be someone who has entered the gate of Secret Mantra.

The manner or method is to take refuge with devoted and respectful body, speech, and mind.

Regarding the particular attitude of taking refuge, you should take refuge by perceiving the guru as a buddha, not abandoning the yidam even at the cost of your life, and continuously making offerings to the dakini.

Regarding the duration of time, you should take refuge from the time of having generated bodhicitta in the empowerment ceremony until attaining the state of a vajra holder.

Regarding the circumstance, you should take refuge by feeling devotion to the Secret Mantra.

As for the purpose or virtues of taking refuge, it has the purpose of making you a suitable vessel for the Secret Mantra and for receiving extraordinary blessings.

Lady Tsogyal asked the master: Concerning the inner way of taking refuge, which trainings does one need to practice?

The master replied: There are eight trainings. First there are the three special trainings.

1. Having taken refuge in the guru, you should not feel ill will toward him or even the intention to deride him.

2. Having taken refuge in the yidam, you should not interrupt the meditation of the yidam's form or its recitation.

3. Having taken refuge in the dakini, you should not break the periodical offering days.

The five general trainings are the following.

1. Consecrate as nectar, the first part of whatever you eat or drink. Offer it visualizing the guru above your head. Offer it, visualizing the yidam in your heart center and the dakini in your navel center. You should train in partaking of food in this way.

2. In whichever direction you go, supplicate the guru, yidam, and dakini. Visualize the guru above the crown of your head. Visualize yourself as the yidam and visualize the dakini and the Dharma protectors as your escorts. This is the training in walking.

3. Even at the cost of your life or limb, you should train in regarding the guru to be as dear as your heart, the yidam as dear as your eyes, and the dakini as dear as your body.

4. No matter what happens, such as sickness, difficulty or ease, joy or sorrow, you should train in supplicating the guru, making offerings to the yidam, and giving feasts and torma to the dakini. Other than that, you should not pursue other means such as soothsaying and shamanistic rituals.

5. Recollecting the virtues of the guru, yidam, and dakini, you should take refuge again and again. By taking refuge in the guru, obstacles are cleared away. By taking refuge in the yidam, the body of mahamudra[3] will be attained. By taking refuge in the dakini, you will receive the siddhis.

Lady Tsogyal asked Master Padma: With which virtues is the inner way of taking refuge endowed?

---

3. The "body of mahamudra" refers to the rainbowlike form of one's personal yidam. See the chapter on the four vidyadhara levels, "Vajrayana Mind Training."

Master Padma replied: By taking refuge in the guru, you are protected from the fetters of conceptual mind. The hindrances of ignorance and stupidity are cleared away. The accumulation of insight and awareness is perfected, and you will receive the accomplishment of spontaneous realization.

By taking refuge in the yidam, you are protected from ordinary perception, the accumualtion of self-existing wisdom will be gathered, and the accomplishment of mahamudra will be attained.

By taking refuge in the dakini, you will be protected from obstacles and evil spirits. The impediment of the poverty of hungry ghosts is cleared away, the accumulation of detachment and freedom from clinging will be perfected, and the accomplishment of the sambhogakaya of great bliss will be attained.

Lady Tsogyal asked Master Padma: What is the actual practice of the inner way of taking refuge?

The master replied: You should first arouse the aspiration toward unexcelled enlightenment. Then visualize the guru, yidam, and dakini upon seats of sun, moon, and lotus in the sky before you and say three times:

> Root of the lineage, lord guru,
> Originator of the siddhis, yidam deity,
> Bestower of excellent blessings, dakini,
> I pay homage to the three roots.

Following that, focus your mind undistractedly upon the guru, yidam, and dakini and repeatedly say:

> I take refuge in the guru, yidam, and dakini.

Then supplicate as follows:

> All gurus, yidams, and dakinis, please bestow upon me the blessings of your body, speech, and mind!
> Please confer the empowerments upon me! Please grant me the supreme and common siddhis! Please extend your kindness to me, your devoted child!

Following that, dissolve the guru into the top of your head, the yidam into your heart center, and the dakini into your navel center.

Lady Tsogyal asked the master: What is the method of taking the inner refuge vow?

The master replied: The ceremony of first taking the refuge vow is as follows. It is important to have received empowerment. Obtaining the empowerment itself is the receiving of refuge. If you do take refuge without receiving empowerment, then make prostrations to and circumambulate the guru, present him with flowers, and say:

> Master, please listen to me. Assembly of yidam deities, gathering of mandala deities, dakinis, and retinue, please listen to me. From this very moment until attaining the supreme vidyadhara level of mahamudra, I, _____, take refuge in the root of the lineage, all the sublime and holy gurus.
>
> I take refuge in the source of accomplishment, all the assemblies of yidam deities.
>
> I take refuge in the bestowers of excellent blessings, all the dakinis.

The refuge vow is obtained after repeating this three times.

That was the ceremony of taking the vow. I have explained the inner way of taking refuge.

THE SECRET WAY OF TAKING REFUGE

Lady Tsogyal, the Princess of Kharchen, asked the master: Concerning the secret way of taking refuge, in what object does one take refuge? What type of person takes refuge? Through which manner or method does one take refuge? With what particular attitude does one take refuge? For what duration of time does one take refuge? By which circumstance does one take refuge? What purpose or virtue is entailed?

The master replied: As to the objects of the secret way of taking refuge, you should take refuge in the view, meditation, and action.

The type of person who takes this refuge should be someone of the highest faculties who desires to attain enlightenment.

As to the manner or method, you should take refuge by means of the view, meditation, action, and fruition. That is to say, you take refuge with the view possessing confidence, the meditation possessing experience, and the action possessing equal taste.

As to the particular attitude, the view free from craving means not to desire either to attain buddhahood or to cast away samsara. The meditation free from fixation on concreteness and without falling into partiality cannot be described by any ordinary words. The conduct free from accepting and rejecting is devoid of falling into any category whatsoever.

The duration of time is to take refuge until attaining enlightenment.

The circumstance is to take refuge without desiring further rebirth.

The purpose or virtue is to attain complete enlightenment within this very lifetime.

Lady Tsogyal asked: Concerning the secret way of taking refuge, in which trainings does one need to practice?

Master Padma replied: First there are the three special trainings:

1. Concerning the view possessing realization: You should train in gaining the confidence that there is no buddhahood elsewhere to achieve, since all sentient beings and buddhas have the same basis. You should train in gaining the confidence that appearance and emptiness are inseparable, through realizing that appearances and mind are without difference.

2. Concerning training in the meditation possessing experience: Do not place your mind facing outward, do not concentrate it inward, but train in letting it rest naturally, freely, and free from reference point.

3. As to the action: Train in uninterrupted experience. Although at all times of walking, moving around, lying down, and sitting there is nothing to be meditated upon, train in not being distracted for even an instant.

The following are the seven general trainings.

1. Do not abandon your master even though you realize your mind to be the buddha.

2. Do not interrupt conditioned roots of virtue even though you realize appearances to be mind.

3. Shun even the most subtle evil deed, even though you have no fear for the hells.

4. Do not denigrate any of the teachings, even though you do not entertain any hope for enlightenment.

5. Do not be conceited or boastful even though you realize superior samadhis.

6. Do not cease feeling compassion for sentient beings, even though you understand self and other to be nondual.

7. Train by practicing in retreat places, even though you realize samsara and nirvana to be nondual.

Lady Tsogyal asked the nirmanakaya master: Concerning the secret way of taking refuge, in what manner does it protect and with what virtues is it endowed?

Master Padma replied: Having taken refuge in the view, you are protected from both eternalism and nihilism. The hindrances of wrong views and fixation are cleared away, the accumulation of the luminous dharmata is perfected, and the unceasing siddhis of body, speech, and mind will be attained.

Having taken refuge in the meditation, the view will also protect the meditation. The obstacles of deep clinging and habitual tendencies are cleared away, the accumulation of nondual unity gathered, and the siddhis of confidence and primordial liberation will be attained.

Having taken refuge in the action, you are protected from perverted conduct and the view of nihilism. The obstacles of hypocrisy and foolishness are cleared away, the accumulation of nonattachment during bustle is perfected, and the siddhi of turning whatever is experienced into realization will be attained.

Lady Tsogyal asked Master Padma: What is the actual practice of the secret way of taking refuge?

The master replied: The view, in natural ease, should be free from craving and devoid of partiality and extremes.

The meditation should be free from fixating on concreteness and reference points. It cannot be expressed by any ordinary words whatsoever.

That is to say, do not place your mind facing outward, do not concentrate it inward, rest in naturalness free from reference point.

Rest undistractedly in the state of unceasing experience at the time of walking, moving around, lying, or sitting.

The feelings of fulfillment or exhilaration, feeling void, blissful, or clear, are all temporary experiences. They should never be regarded as marvelous.

When states of mind that are agitated, obscured, or drowsy occur, use these experiences as training. Whatever occurs, such as these, do not regard them as defects.

Lady Tsogyal asked: What is the method of taking the vow of the secret way of taking refuge?

The master replied: Prostrating to and circumambulating the master, present him with flowers. The disciple should assume the cross-legged posture and with compassion take the vow of cultivating bodhicitta for the benefit of self and others.

Then, placing the gaze firmly in the sky and without moving the eyeballs, rest your awareness—vivid, awake, bright, and all-pervasive—free from fixation on perceiver or the perceived. That itself is the view possessing confidence, the meditation possessing experience, and the action possessing companionship! Thus it should be pointed out. Meditate then as mentioned above.

This was the explanation of the secret way of taking refuge.

The nirmanakaya master Padma said: This was my oral instruction in which the outer, inner, and secret teachings, the higher and lower views, and the vehicles of mantra and philosophy[4] are condensed into a single root within the outer, inner, and secret way of taking refuge.

---

4. "Mantra" means Vajrayana, and the "vehicle of philosophy" includes both Hinayana and Mahayana.

When you apply it accordingly, you will turn toward Dharma practice, your Dharma practice will become the path, and your path will ripen into fruition. Princess of Kharchen, you should understand this to be so.

This completes the teachings on practicing the taking of refuge as one's path.

SAMAYA. SEAL, SEAL, SEAL.

ༀ་པ་རཀ་སཾ་ཀའ་ཉ་སྣ྅ༀ

Bodhicitta

The Teachings on Taking the Arousing of Bodhicitta as the Path

The great master Padmakara is an emanation of Buddha Amitabha. Having trained his mind in the numerous Mahayana sutras, he loves all sentient beings as a mother loves her only child. Acting always for the welfare of others, he is the steersman who delivers all samsaric beings to nirvana. Without being asked he gives instruction to all those to be tamed. Endowed with great compassion he is the king of all bodhisattvas.

When he was staying in the Lion Fortress Cave at Monkha, I, Lady Tsogyal of Kharchen, aroused bodhicitta, the mind set on supreme enlightenment. Having offered a mandala of precious substances to the great master, I made this petition: Emaho! Great master, you have taught that having cultivated love and compassion for all beings, the sole importance in the Mahayana teaching is to train in bodhicitta. This being so, how should we engage in the training of bodhicitta?

The master replied: Tsogyal, if, having entered the Mahayana, you do not train in bodhicitta, you will fall into the lower vehicles. Therefore it is essential to always arouse the mind that is set on supreme enlightenment and to exert yourself in the trainings of benefiting others.

Countless detailed explanations of that have been given in the sutras and tantras of the Mahayana. When bodhicitta is explained concisely in accordance with these teachings, it is divided into three sections: the outer training, the inner training, and the secret training.

THE OUTER TRAINING IN BODHICITTA

Lady Tsogyal asked: What are the methods of the outer training? The master replied: There are twelve points to the outer training.

1. The essence of training in bodhicitta
2. Its divisions
3. Its definition
4. The characteristics of the person
5. The object from whom you take the vow
6. The ceremony for taking it
7. The benefits of the training
8. The reason for training
9. The shortcomings of not training
10. The precepts
11. The dividing line between losing and possessing it
12. The method for repairing it if damaged

She asked: How are these points you have described?

1. THE ESSENCE

The master replied: The essence of arousing bodhicitta is the desire to attain unexcelled enlightenment together with the vow to do so in order to liberate all sentient beings from samsara.

2. THE DIVISIONS

The sutras describe many classifications of divisions, but in short, there are two kinds: aspiration and application. The aspiration is the wish to accomplish the welfare of beings, but that alone is not sufficient. It is important to actually engage in benefiting all sentient beings.

It seems to be quite difficult for prejudiced people who are not free from egotism to give rise to bodhicitta.

3. THE DEFINITION

The definition of bodhicitta is the arising in oneself of an altruistic attitude that has not previously arisen.

This attitude will not arise in beings who have not gathered the accumulations.

4. THE CHARACTERISTICS OF THE PERSON

The person who engages in the training of bodhicitta should possess certain characteristics. He should aspire toward the teaching of the Mahayana, unlike the shravakas and pratyekabuddhas. Due to great intelligence, he should be totally free from doubt. He should have taken refuge in a master and in the Three Jewels and should feel weary of incorrect or inferior teachings. He should be naturally peaceful and gentle.

The people of Tibet are hostile toward the Dharma, the ministers are evil minded, the king is gullible; there are only a few who are suitable recipients for the Mahayana teachings. Tsogyal, be free from partiality toward friend and enemy.

5. THE OBJECT

The object from whom you take the bodhicitta vow should be a master who has the Mahayana aspiration and whose mind is filled with love and compassion. He should be a teacher who does not act for the benefit of himself for even an instant, and who observes his precepts without transgressions.

In this dark age, one will fall into the hands of Mara unless one follows a qualified master.

6. THE CEREMONY

The ceremony for taking the bodhicitta vow is as follows. Having arranged an extensive display of offerings before the Three Jewels on the fifteenth or the eighth of the waxing moon in an auspicious year and month, pay respect to the sangha. Offer a ganachakra to the yidam. Make extensive torma offerings to the dakinis, Dharma protectors, and elemental spirits. Give away all your possessions and gather a vast amount of merit.

That same evening, offer the initiation fee to the master. With respect for the master, the disciple should gather the accumulations by means of the seven pure aspects.[1]

In particular, you should confess misdeeds as follows. Visualize the syllable A at the crown of your head. By means of the light streaming forth from it, establish all sentient beings in the enlightenment of the buddhas and make offerings to all noble beings. By means of the light being absorbed back into the A, absorb the nectar of the siddhis of all the noble ones, which then dissolves into your body, speech, and mind, and burns away all of your misdeeds and obscurations. Imagining that, recite A 108 times.

Imagine that the light radiating from the HUNG in the heart of the wisdom being in the master's heart center dissolves into your body, speech, and mind and thereby burns away all misdeeds. Thinking this, recite HUNG 108 times.

Then follows the verbal confession. Remembering all misdeeds accumulated since beginningless samsara, recite this confession three times with remorse.

> Vajra master and all vidyadharas, pay heed to me!
>
> Assembly of yidam deities together with your retinue of peaceful and wrathful buddhas, pay heed to me!
>
> Victorious ones of the ten directions together with your sons, pay heed to me!
>
> Mother dakinis guarding the teachings together with the Dharma protectors, pay heed to me!
>
> In the presence of those who are worthy of veneration, I, _____ , remorsefully confess all the evil karmic actions I have accumulated by the power of erroneous thinking by means of body, speech, and mind, through committing unvirtuous actions and misdeeds, causing others to commit them or rejoicing in their doing so, from beginningless lifetimes to this very day.

Then resolve not to further proliferate misdeeds. Repeat the above supplication and then say three times:

---

1. The seven-branch practice of prostrating to the Three Jewels, confessing negative actions, making offerings, rejoicing in the virtue of others, requesting to turn the wheel of Dharma, beseeching to not pass into nirvana, and dedicating the merit to the enlightenment of all sentient beings.

Just as the tathagatas and their sons of the past, by means of the perfect life-examples of the paths and bhumis, turned away from unvirtuous actions and misdeeds, so will I, _____, from this very moment until reaching the essence of enlightenment, turn away from committing misdeeds through erroneous thinking. I vow to henceforth refrain from them.

The Actual Arousing of Bodhicitta

This has two parts. The first is for the beginner to arouse the bodhicitta of aspiration.

From the core of his heart the disciple should arouse the genuine attitude of thinking: In order to save all the sentient beings of samsara from the ocean of suffering, I will attain unexcelled enlightenment!

At the end of repeating the above supplication he should say three times:

> With the attitude of regarding all sentient beings as being my fathers and mothers, my brothers and sisters, my sons and daughters, or my teachers and Dharma friends, I, _____, from this very day until reaching the essence of enlightenment, will generate the firm intention of liberating all beings who have not been liberated. I will cross over the ones who have not crossed over, I will relieve the ones who are not relieved, and I will establish in the nondwelling state of enlightenment of the buddhas all beings who have not passed beyond suffering.[2]

Secondly, for arousing the bodhicitta of application, form the thought: From this very moment and for as long as samsara is not emptied, without being distracted for even a single moment, I will accomplish the welfare of beings in manifold ways. Repeat the above supplication, after which you should say three times:

> From this very moment until samsara is emptied, I, _____, will persistently generate the firm intention to gradually train, carry out, and perfect the six paramitas and the four means of

---

2. Liberating the beings in the three lower realms to a state in which they can practice the Dharma; helping the beings of the three higher realms to cross the ocean of samsara and attain emancipation; relieving the aspirant bodhisattvas with the attainment of the bhumis.

magnetizing. Just as the buddhas of the past and all the bodhisattvas by means of the perfect life-examples of the paths and
bhumis were endowed with the root and branch vows, in that
way I also will train, carry out, and perfect them. Please regard
me as a bodhisattva.

The master then says, So be it! and the disciple, It is good! It is
meaningful! After having repeated the above three times, one has
obtained the vow.

In order to keep the vow unimpaired from that moment on, the
master should instruct the disciple in the precepts. The disciple
should then offer a gift and perform an extensive offering of thanksgiving.

From that moment on it is of the greatest importance to continuously exert oneself in arousing bodhicitta and in the trainings of
bodhicitta, like the steady flow of a river.

7. THE BENEFITS

The benefits of training in the bodhicitta you have thus developed
are as follows. Elevated above the shravakas and pratyekabuddhas,
you are included in the assembly of Mahayana practitioners. Your
disturbing emotions, misdeeds, and obscurations are all annihilated
from their very root. All the virtuous actions of your body, speech,
and mind become causes for what is meaningful and a vast gathering
of merit will be perfected in your being. You will always be watched
over by the buddhas and bodhisattvas and the great protectors of the
Dharma. All sentient beings will love you as their own child and find
you beautiful to behold. You will never be separated from the
Mahayana teachings.

In short, you will quickly accomplish the superior qualities of
buddhahood and awaken to true and complete enlightenment. Thus
the qualities are inconceivable. Therefore be persistent in just this.

8. THE REASONS FOR TRAINING

It may be sufficient to attain liberation by yourself alone, so why
should you liberate all sentient beings from samsara? Since all beings

are your own parents, your debt of gratitude is inconceivably great, and so you need to train in order to repay their kindness.

Their kindness consists in forming the basis for your life and body; raising you from childhood with the best food and drink; undertaking all kinds of pain and difficulties for your benefit; cherishing you as higher than themselves, more important even than their own hearts.

Moreover, they have endowed you with wealth and possessions, educated you, connected you to the sacred Dharma and so forth. Because of the inconceivably great kindness of these parents, you must liberate them all from samsara. Since all sentient beings have the basic cause, the essence of enlightenment, you are also connected with them and so you must liberate them all from samsara.

Tsogyal, if you desire happiness for yourself alone, you have no connection to perfect buddhahood.

9. THE DEFECTS OF NOT TRAINING

The defects of not training are as follows. Having fallen to the level of being a shravaka and pratyekabuddha, you are hindered in attaining the great enlightenment; all the actions you perform become futile; all the merit you have accumulated in the past will be exhausted; you will always be hampered by spirits; others will feel hostile and dislike you. In short, your wishes will never be fulfilled and so forth. Thus there are countless shortcomings.

Tsogyal, how silly it is to expect to be a Mahayana follower without possessing bodhicitta.

10. THE PRECEPTS

There are two types of precepts to observe. For the precepts of the bodhicitta of aspiration you must train again and again in bodhicitta with the intention to never forsake sentient beings. The bodhicitta of aspiration is impaired if:

> ° preceded by the intention to reject another sentient being, you get angry or physically hit another person and allow one day to pass without applying an antidote;

° preceded by the intention to deceive your master, teacher, vajra friend, or anyone else worthy of respect, you deceive them and let one day pass without applying an antidote;

° you cause someone to regret a vast root of merit he has created, which is an object for rejoicing and not for feeling regret. This occurs when, preceded by the intention to make him feel remorse, you say, "There is something superior to this! This is not excellent!";

° motivated by anger, you utter a sentence of criticism to a bodhisattva who has developed bodhicitta;

° without compassion, you deceive another sentient being.

These deeds are called the five perverted actions if you allow one day to pass without counteracting them with an antidote. Give them up as they will cause you to lose your vow of aspiration.

Tsogyal, you can be ruined by taking many precepts which you do not keep.

There are, moreover, five actions to which you should adhere.

1. As an antidote to showing anger or beating sentient beings, you should always be peaceful and gentle, and try to help them.

2. As an antidote to deceiving someone worthy of respect, you should be conscientious and never lie even at the cost of your life.

3. As an antidote to causing others to feel regret, establish all sentient beings in the virtue that leads to the great enlightenment of the buddhas.

4. As an antidote to criticizing others out of anger, you should praise all followers of the Mahayana while regarding them as your teachers.

5. As an antidote to deceiving sentient beings, you should take your own mind as witness, and with pure intention, follow those who are stable.

Adhere to these deeds and you will be a holder of the teachings of Shakyamuni even though you are born as a woman.

Secondly, the precepts of the bodhicitta of application will be explained under three points: (1) the ten nonvirtues to be abandoned, (2) the ten virtuous actions that are the antidotes, and (3) the ten paramitas that are to be engaged in.

The Ten Nonvirtues

Among the ten nonvirtues, there are first the three physical deeds: killing, taking what is not given, and engaging in sexual misconduct.

Killing

The essence of killing is to interrupt the continuation of life. There are three types enacted by the three poisons.

1. Killing out of desire means to slaughter animals due to desire for their meat, skin, and so forth.

2. Killing out of anger means, for example, to murder another with a vicious intention.

3. Killing out of delusion means to kill without intention, for example, when a child kills a bird or an ant dies by being trodden on.

Sentient beings who are not free from the three poisons have no happiness.

The act of killing is completed when committed by means of the following four aspects.

1. The preceding thought of intending "I will do such a misdeed!"
2. The deliberate engagement in the act and pursuing it with effort
3. The actual deed of killing, experiencing the act
4. The conclusion of rejoicing in the act without feeling regret

The results of killing appear in three ways.

1. The result of ripening is that by killing out of desire you will mainly be reborn as a hungry ghost, by killing out of anger you will mostly be reborn in the hells, and by killing out of delusion you will mainly be reborn as an animal.

2. The result of the dominant action is that, dominated by the former unvirtuous action, you will have a short life span and much sickness even if you take rebirth as a human being.

3. The result corresponding to the cause is that you will take pleasure in the act of killing, due to your former habitual tendencies.

Tsogyal, therefore we should not commit these actions. The sutras teach that if you put effort into abandoning these actions you will turn away from the previous result of ripening, the result corresponding to the cause, and the dominant result. Then you will attain the abundant happiness of gods and men.

Taking What Is Not Given

The essence of the second physical nonvirtue, taking what is not given, is the act of making another person's possession your own.

This nonvirtue includes taking by force, for example robbing in open daylight, taking by sneak such as stealing unnoticed, and taking by deceit, for example dishonesty with weights and scales.

Tsogyal, people who have not turned away from desire possess no happiness.

Just as before, this action is consummated when four aspects are complete, and the results are again of three types.

1. The result of ripening is that you fall into the three lower realms according to whether the act is done to a greater, medium, or lesser degree. In particular, you will be reborn as a hungry ghost.

2. The dominant result will be that, even if you are reborn as a human being, you will have few possessions and encounter a lot of thievery and robbery.

3. The result corresponding to the cause is that, due to this unwholesome habitual tendency being accumulated in the all-ground, you will delight in taking what is not given in future lives.

Tsogyal, if you give up committing such actions you will have three results. You will obtain the opposite of the previous three results, such as being reborn in the forms of gods and men, having much wealth and so forth.

Sexual Misconduct

The essence of the third physical nonvirtue, sexual misconduct, is the act of engaging in intercourse with an object of desire with whom one has no authority to do so.

When divided, there are the following kinds.

1. It is unsuitable for a commoner to have intercourse with someone under the guardianship of a king, such as his queen.

2. It is unsuitable to have intercourse with someone prohibited by the law.

3. In India, it is unsuitable to have casual intercourse with someone under the guardianship of parents, since men and women not in their own household are protected by their parents.

4. It is unsuitable to have intercourse with someone protected by "civilized principles," which means someone with whom it is shameful, such as a mother or a sister.

5. It is unsuitable to have intercourse with someone under the guardianship of the sacred Dharma, such as the guru's consort, an ordained person, and so forth.

Lustful people do not enter the path of liberation. Tsogyal, apply the antidote.

There are also occasions on which it is unsuitable to have intercourse even with your rightful companion.

1. It is unsuitable to have intercourse at an inappropriate time such as on the full moon, new moon, and the eighth day.

2. It is unsuitable to have intercourse in an inappropriate location, such as in the presence of a shrine for the Three Jewels.

3. It is unsuitable to have intercourse in an inappropriate orifice, such as engaging in the manner of animals.

Tsogyal, in general people who have not abandoned the life of householders are trapped in the prison of Mara.

As before, the act of sexual misconduct is consummated by means of the four completing aspects, and again there are three types of results.

1. Through the result of ripening you will be reborn in the three lower realms. Even if you do take rebirth in the higher realms, you will have fights with your spouse and so forth.

2. The dominant result is that even in future lives your helpers, spouse, and so forth will be unresponsive and show various acts of ingratitude.

3. The result corresponding to the cause is that your unwholesome

habitual tendencies will cause you to take pleasure in sexual misconduct.

Tsogyal, if you give up these acts and refrain from engaging in them, you will obtain the opposites of their results, so abandoning them is of great importance.

Secondly, there are four types of verbal nonvirtues.

Telling Lies

The essence of the first, telling lies, is to verbally state that something untrue is true.

When divided, there are the following kinds.

1. There are lies that neither benefit nor harm, such as the lies of an old, senile man.

2. There are lies that do benefit or harm, such as benefiting one person while harming another.

3. The "lie of having supreme human qualities" means that you claim to possess qualities in your stream of being such as higher perceptions, when you do not.

Tsogyal, do not utter a lot of thoughtless words.

As before, the act of telling lies is consummated by means of the four completing aspects, and again there are three types of results.

1. The result of ripening is that you fall into the lower realms.

2. The dominant result is that even if you are reborn as a human, your voice will hold no power.

3. The result corresponding to the cause is that in future lives you will again delight in telling lies.

Tsogyal, if you give up these acts you will obtain the opposites of their results, so abandoning them is of great importance.

Divisive Talk

The essence of the second verbal nonvirtue, divisive talk, is the act of separating people who are good friends.

When divided, there are the following types.

1. Public divisive talk by talking directly to someone's face
2. Indirect divisive talk by talking in a roundabout way

3. Private divisive talk by talking to others individually

Tsogyal, people who cannot keep their lips tight will have no happiness.

The four completing aspects are just as before, and there are again three types of results.

1. The result of ripening is that you will fall into the three lower realms.

2. The dominant result is that, even if you take rebirth as a human being, you will have few friends and many arguments. You will always have many regrets, be disliked by everyone, and whatever you utter will be ineffective.

3. The result corresponding to the cause is that in future lives you will again take pleasure in divisive talk.

Tsogyal, if we abandon such acts we will attain the opposites of their results, so it is important to abandon them.

Idle Gossip

The essence of the third verbal nonvirtue, idle gossip, is to waste free time.

When divided, there are the following types:

1. Shamanistic incantations
2. Storytelling and word games
3. Bantering conversation

Just as before, it is consummated by the four aspects, and will have these three types of results.

1. The result of ripening is that you will fall into the three lower realms.

2. The dominant result is that, even if you are reborn as a human being, your words will be undignified, babbling, and unconnected.

3. The result corresponding to the cause is that in future lives you will again take pleasure in uttering idle gossip.

Tsogyal, if you give up these acts you will attain the opposite of their results, so do not be fond of pointless chatter.

Harsh Words

The essence of the fourth verbal nonvirtue, harsh words, is talk that hurts another person.

When divided, there are the following kinds.

1. Exposing someone's faults in public
2. Hurting someone indirectly
3. Uttering in private something that will hurt another person

Tsogyal, the fire of harsh words burns the heart of both yourself and others. The weapon of harsh words kills the life force of liberation.

This act is consummated by the four completing aspects, and has the following three types of results.

1. The result of ripening is to be reborn in the three lower realms.

2. The dominant result is that, even if you take rebirth as a human being, whatever you say will be offensive to others and you will always appear to irritate them.

3. The result corresponding to the cause is that you will be fond of speaking harsh words.

Tsogyal, if you abandon these actions you will attain the results of their opposites. The sentient beings of the dark age have no happiness.

Thirdly, there are three mental nonvirtues.

Covetousness

The essence of the first, covetousness, is attachment to something excellent.

When divided, there are the following types:

1. Refraining from giving away your own possessions
2. Desiring to make others' possessions belong to yourself
3. Attachment to something excellent that belongs neither to oneself nor to others

Tsogyal, do not hold on to ownership of material things. Dharma practitioners with no understanding of impermanence have no happiness.

This action is consummated by the four aspects, and has the following three results.

1. The result of ripening is rebirth in the three lower realms.

2. The dominant result is that, even if you take rebirth as a human being, you will always live in an unpleasant area where there is hunger and thirst.

3. The result corresponding to the cause is that in future lives you will take pleasure in covetousness.

Tsogyal, it is therefore essential to abandon these actions.

Ill Will

The essence of the second mental nonvirtue, ill will, is an attitude of hostility.

When divided, there are the following types:

1. Ill will resulting from anger
2. Ill will resulting from resentment
3. Ill will resulting from jealousy

Tsogyal, do not commit mental actions that hurt yourself and harm others.

This act is consummated by the four aspects, and has the following three types of results.

1. The result of ripening is to take rebirth in the lower realms.

2. The dominant result is that, even if you are reborn as a human, others are unjustifiably hostile toward you and constantly you meet with enmity and lawsuits.

3. The result corresponding to the cause is that you will develop a malicious frame of mind.

Tsogyal, if you do not give up ill will you can practice neither Hinayana nor Mahayana.

Wrong Views

The essence of the third mental nonvirtue, wrong views, is to exaggerate or denigrate.

When divided, there are the following kinds.

1. The wrong view of holding the non-Buddhist beliefs of eternalism or nihilism
2. The wrong view of holding a rule or ritual to be paramount, such as "asceticism of dogs and chickens"[3]
3. The wrong view of holding the belief of the "transitory collection"[4]

Tsogyal, there are few who understand the difference between Dharma and non-Dharma.

These actions are consummated by the four aspects, and produce the following three results.

1. The result of ripening is to take rebirth in the three lower realms.

2. The dominant result is that, even if you are reborn as a human being, you will take birth in a place such as in an uncivilized border tribe, where you will not even hear the name of the Three Jewels.

3. The result corresponding to the cause is that the habitual tendencies of holding wrong views will solidify in your all-ground, after which you will be fond of holding wrong views.

Tsogyal, all noble beings denounce these ten nonvirtues. They are renounced by all learned people. They are not to be committed even by those who seek to attain the special splendor and wealth of gods and humans, so give them up.

There are many people who do not recognize good from evil, but those who do have entered the Buddha's teachings. To commit nonvirtue while knowing well the cause and effect of virtuous actions and misdeeds is to be no different from an animal.

Lady Tsogyal asked: When abandoning these actions, what are the results one will attain?

The master replied: As the result of ripening you will be reborn among gods and humans. Like Brahma your voice will be melodious,

---

3. A Hindu system claiming that liberation can be attained by imitating the conduct of animals.

4. The mistaken view that an ego or self-entity is inherently existent within the continuity of the five aggregates.

like Indra your body will be more beautiful than that of others, and like a universal monarch you will have great wealth.

As the dominant result you will hold great learning, you will be very intelligent, and you will meet with the Dharma of the Buddha's teachings. Ultimately you will attain the three levels of enlightenment.

As the result corresponding to the cause you will, in all future lifetimes, exert yourself in abandoning the ten nonvirtues.

Lady Tsogyal asked: Concerning these ten nonvirtues, is there any difference in the severity of evil?

The master replied: Yes, there are differences. In general, there is the division in terms of the disturbing emotion.

1. Through committing the ten nonvirtues out of anger, you will be reborn as a hell-being.

2. When the nonvirtues are committed out of desire, you will be reborn as a hungry ghost.

3. When the nonvirtues are committed out of delusion, you will be reborn as an animal.

There is also a difference in severity in terms of the object.

1. By committing the ten nonvirtues toward a special object, you will be reborn as a hell-being.

2. By committing them toward an ordinary object, you will be reborn as a hungry ghost.

3. By committing them toward an inferior object, you will be reborn as an animal.

In particular, among the different types of killing, the most severe evil ripening stems from taking the life of a bodhisattva who has developed bodhicitta.

Among the different types of taking what is not given, the greatest misdeed is to steal that which belongs to the Three Jewels.

Among the different types of sexual misconduct, the greatest misdeed is to have forced intercourse with an arhant.

Among the different types of telling lies, the greatest misdeed is to deceive a master or a venerable member of the sangha.

Among the different types of divisive talk, the greatest misdeed is to cause a schism in the sangha.

Among the different types of harsh words, the greatest misdeed is to speak unpleasantly to a member of the sangha.

Among the different types of idle gossip, the greatest misdeed is to disturb the mind of a monk or someone practicing the nature of nondual meditaion.

Among the different types of covetousness, the greatest misdeed is to crave the funds donated to the Three Jewels.

Among the different types of ill will, the greatest misdeed is to plan committing the "five deeds with immediate results."

Among the different types of wrong views, the greatest misdeed is to disparage the true meaning.

Tsogyal, you should not commit any of these actions even at the cost of your life.

Generally speaking, there are also differences among the ten nonvirtues.

1. Through killing, divisive talk, harsh words, and ill will, you will be reborn as a hell-being.

2. Through sexual misconduct, taking what is not given, and covetousness, you will be reborn as a hungry ghost.

3. Through telling lies, idle gossip, and holding wrong views, you will be reborn as an animal.

The Ten Virtues

Lady Tsogyal asked the master: How should one practice the ten virtues, the antidotes that are to be adopted?

The master replied: The ten virtues have four topics.

1. The essence is a pure action of body, speech, or mind that produces the truly high.[5]

2. The definition of *virtuous action* is that action which, when correctly committed by a person who has obtained the freedoms and riches, yields the result of a desired happiness.

3. The divisions are the virtues that are the opposites of the ten nonvirtues: to save lives, to be tremendously generous, to abide in

---

5. The term "truly high" simply refers to a rebirth in the three higher realms within samsara: human, demigods, and gods.

pure living, to speak truthfully, to reconcile strife, to speak gently and with discipline, to speak meaningfully, to be loving toward all beings, to be unattached, and to be free from doubt about the results of actions and the definitive meaning.

4. The following are the ten supports that cause the virtues to remain in your stream of being: to have faith in the true teachings, to keep self-respect and pure conscience, to refrain from gambling and quarreling, to refrain from watching market gatherings, to always act conscientiously, to cast away laziness, to not associate with immoral friends, to train in the pliancy of body, speech, and mind, to cultivate the four-fold spheres of perception, and in particular to focus your mind on the path of noble beings.

Tsogyal, by acting in these ways, there is no doubt that you will attain the results of the truly high.

The Ten Paramitas

Thirdly, for engaging in the actions of the ten paramitas, there are five topics.

1. The general essence is that which has the nature of the path for accomplishing unexcelled enlightenment.

2. The definition of *paramita* is that which causes you to reach *(ita)* to the great nirvana, the other shore *(param)* of the ocean of samsara.

3. The function is to perfect the two accumulations and accomplish the welfare of sentient beings.

4. There are two kinds of divisions; general and specific. The general division is the six paramitas of generosity, discipline, patience, diligence, concentration, and discriminating knowledge.

Specifically, generosity has three types: the giving of Dharma teachings, the giving of material things, and the giving of protection against fear.

Discipline also has three types: the discipline of refraining from misdeeds, the discipline of gathering virtuous qualities, and the discipline of benefiting sentient beings. In other words, these disciplines are observed by refraining from the ten nonvirtues, by the six paramitas, and by the four means of magnetizing.

Patience also has three types: the patience of being unconcerned about undergoing suffering when renouncing samsara, the patience of undertaking hardship in order to benefit beings, and the patience of keeping confidence in the Dharma, which means to refrain from fearing the profound nature.

Diligence also has three types: the diligence of applying the Mahayana teachings, the armorlike diligence of repelling adversity, and the relentless diligence of accomplishing the buddhahood of perfect omniscience.

Meditation also has three types: the meditation that focuses on the correct mundane path, the meditation that focuses on the supramundane path, and the general meditation that takes both as focus.

Knowledge again has three types: the knowledge that realizes conditioned things to be beyond focus, the knowledge that realizes the innate nature to be beyond focus, and the knowledge that realizes that all phenomena are beyond duality and transcend words, thought, and description.

You should know that in order to assimilate each method within your stream of being, you must have four paramitas complete.

To vanquish stinginess and poverty through the generosity of not expecting a reward is the paramita of strength.

To give while being free from the intentions of ordinary people and the Hinayana is the paramita of method.

To give with the thought, May I interrupt the poverty of myself and all sentient beings! is the paramita of aspiration.

To give with the total purity of the three spheres is the paramita of wisdom.[6]

Similarly, to vanquish nonvirtue with the discipline of not desiring samsaric results is the paramita of strength.

To observe your vows while being free from the eight worldly concerns is the paramita of method.

To wish, May the immoral behavior of all sentient beings be interrupted! while not desiring the states of gods and men for yourself alone, is the paramita of aspiration.

---

6. The three spheres are the concepts of subject, object, and action.

To embrace that with the nonconceptualization of the three spheres is the paramita of wisdom.

To vanquish anger by behaving equally to everyone is the paramita of strength.

Not to hold a worldly purpose such as deceit and hypocrisy is the paramita of method.

Not to desire rebirth in a beautiful body of gods or humans for yourself alone, but to wish, May the ugliness of all sentient beings be pacified! is the paramita of aspiration.

To embrace that with the nonconceptualization of the three spheres is the paramita of wisdom.

To vanquish laziness with the diligence of keeping the faults and qualities in mind is the paramita of strength.

Not to hold a worldly purpose, such as expecting to be held in faith by others, is the paramita of method.

To wish, May all beings bring an end to laziness and exert themselves on the true path! is the paramita of aspiration.

To embrace that with the nonconceptualization of the three spheres is the paramita of wisdom.

To vanquish distraction through the concentration that has transcended the formless realms is the paramita of strength.

To practice for the sake of accomplishing the qualities of unexcelled enlightenment, with no desire for the states of gods or men, is the paramita of method.

To wish, May the distraction of all sentient beings be interrupted! is the paramita of aspiration.

To refrain from conceptualizing the three spheres is the paramita of wisdom.

To vanquish the constructs of distinguishing attributes with the knowledge of emptiness endowed with the nature of compassion is the paramita of strength.

To be inseparable from that throughout the three times is the paramita of method.

To wish, May I and all others realize the true meaning! is the paramita of aspiration.

To recognize the fact that since the beginning, your mind essence has had the nature of this knowledge is the paramita of wisdom.

Tsogyal, practice in this way undistractedly.

5. The result of practicing the ten paramitas is that you will be liberated from the lower realms and, attaining the special level of gods or men, you will perfect the paths and swiftly attain buddhahood, after which you will become a great guide liberating sentient beings from samsara.

11. THE DIVIDING LINE BETWEEN LOSING AND POSSESSING THE VOW

The moment of obtaining the bodhicitta vow is as follows. Having gathered a vast accumulation of merit, when you give rise to the thought that you must accomplish the genuine welfare of beings through fully purifying your mind, you obtain the bodhicitta vow at the end of the third utterance of the complete ritual.

The moment of losing the bodhicitta vow is when you give rise to wrong views or denounce the Three Jewels, thus violating the trainings. It is therefore essential to exert yourself while keeping mindfulness and conscientiousness on guard.

12. THE METHOD FOR REPAIRING WHEN DAMAGED

If you damage the root precepts, you must retake the vow as instructed before. If you have damaged the branch precepts, you must confess that in the presence of the master or the Three Jewels.

THE INNER BODHICITTA

Lady Tsogyal asked the master: How should one train when arousing bodhicitta in the inner way?

The master replied: For this there are also twelve points of training.

1. THE ESSENCE

The essence is to arouse the intention to help those beings who do not realize that the innate nature, the true meaning, is devoid of constructs.

2. THE DEFINITION

Without being dependent upon "outer" actions of body or speech, it is called "inner" because it is developed exclusively by your mind.

3. THE DIVISIONS

There are two divisions: aspiration and application.

The aspiration is to wish that sentient beings who have not realized this nature may realize it. Just to sit and mutter this is not enough; you must exert yourself in the means for making all sentient beings realize it.

Tsogyal, as long as you are not free from dualistic fixation the application is rather difficult.

4. THE CHARACTERISTICS OF THE PRACTITIONER

In addition to earlier explanations, the characterisic of the person who engages in this training is to have only a minor degree of conceptual constructs.

Tsogyal, let your mind take some rest!

5. THE OBJECT FROM WHOM IT IS TAKEN

You should receive it from a master who has realized the nature of the twofold selflessness through training in the three types of knowledge, and is thus free from the eight worldly concerns.

Tsogyal, a master is essential for entering the gate of the Mahayana teachings.

6. THE CEREMONY FOR RECEIVING

Free yourself from the three spheres of concepts, give up concerns for all worldly activities, and thus request the true oral instructions.

7. THE BENEFITS OF THE TRAINING

Your will rise far above the Hinayana and erroneous paths. Thus it has the effect of abandoning all thoughts of selfishness and dualistic fixation, and of realizing the nature of selflessness.

8. THE REASON FOR THE TRAINING

The reason for training in this inner way of arousing bodhicitta is to establish all sentient beings on the true path, the nature of the twofold selflessness.

9. THE SHORTCOMINGS OF NOT TRAINING

The defect of not training is that you will stray from the nature of selflessness.

For ordinary people whose minds have not been changed by a philosophical school, and for non-Buddhists who have entered an incorrect philosophical school, the self of the individual is regarded as being that which controls and experiences the conditioned five aggregates, twelve sense bases, and eighteen constituents. Moreover, regarding this self as being permanent and concrete, they fixate on it as being friend and enemy, self and other.

Tsogyal, you must pull up this stake of fixation.

The danger of conceptualizing such an individual self is that by apprehending an ego and a self-entity, objects will appear as "something other." By apprehending this duality, you will regard that which benefits the "self" as friend and that which harms the "self" as enemy. Thus the experiences of attachment and aversion will cause you to commit various kinds of unvirtuous actions. Through these actions you will wander in the lower realms and the whole of samsara.

Tsogyal, unless you expel this evil spirit you will find no happiness.

What type of person denounces this self? In general it is denounced by all Buddhists. In particular, the shravakas specifically denounce it. Needless to say, we who have entered the gate of the Mahayana also denounce fixation on the individual self.

It is claimed that the shravakas partially realize the self of phenomena, and that also the pratyekabuddhas do not realize it fully. That is to say, the shravakas mistakenly assert the existence of matter instead of understanding the self of phenomena, and the pratyekabuddhas dwell in the state of fixating on the empty mind-essence instead of understanding the correct meaning.

Tsogyal, as long as you are not free from the beliefs of the lower philosophical schools you will not perceive the true meaning.

The danger of conceptualizing the self of phenomena is that by such assertion and fixation you will give rise to disturbing emotions. These will cause you to wander in samsara. That is pointless effort even if you were to exert yourself for aeons.

What type of person denounces the self of phenomena? In general all Mahayana followers denounce it. In particular, it would be a bad sign if we who have entered the gate of Secret Mantra fixate on partiality, as the followers of the Middle Way also denounce it.

10. THE POINTS TO BE OBSERVED

You should train yourself in the meaning of selflessness, of which there are two kinds, aspiration and application.

The three important points of aspiration to be observed are as follows.

1. To continually form the aspiration of thinking, May all sentient beings always realize the meaning of selflessness!
2. To train yourself three times a day and three times a night in rejoicing in others who meditate on the meaning of selflessness
3. To always train yourself assiduously in not straying from the meaning of selflessness

Secondly, the two points of application to be observed are the outer and the inner.

The four outer trainings are:

1. Not to separate yourself from the master or spiritual friend who teaches the meaning of selflessness until you have realized it
2. To give up partiality concerning dwelling place, country and area, caste, enemy, and friend
3. To study, reflect, and meditate upon the teachings that demonstrate selflessness and emptiness
4. Not to fixate on yourself as being a name, family, or body

The four inner trainings are:

1. Not to apprehend names as being things since all labels and names of outer things have no existence in your mind
2. To acknowledge that everything which comprises the world and the beings within it has no self-nature, although it appears, just like dreams and magic
3. To seek out three times a day and three times a night this mind that fixates on various objects, although nothing whatsoever exists
4. Not to stray from the meaning that is nameless and devoid of extremes. Even though you search your mind, it is not found to be anything whatsoever

It is of utmost importance to train yourself diligently in this way. Through exerting yourself in this way, you will annihilate the evil spirit and turn away from samsara.

11. THE DIVIDING LINE BETWEEN LOSING AND POSSESSING THE VOW

The moment of obtaining the inner bodhicitta vow is when you receive the oral instructions from your master.

The moment of losing it is when you pursue ordinary dualistic fixation without understanding the nonexistence of a self-nature. Since it is lost at that moment, by sure to apply the antidote!

12. THE METHOD FOR REPAIRING WHEN DAMAGED

Train in remaining undistracted from the meaning just explained and you will automatically untie the knot of dualistic fixation.

THE SECRET TRAINING

Lady Tsogyal asked the master: How should one train in the secret arousing of bodhicitta?

The master replied: This has eleven points.

1. THE ESSENCE

The essence of the secret arousing of bodhicitta is to recognize that which is beyond effort since the beginning, the primordial purity of nonarising free from the limitations of thought and description.

2. THE DEFINITION

It is naturally secret from all the lower vehicles since it lies beyond that which can be indicated by words or thought of by the mind.

3. THE DIVISIONS

When divided, there are two positions: asserting the universal purity to be nonmeditation and asserting the spontaneously present nature to be primordially perfected as nonmeditation. You should be free from any partiality concerning this.[7]

4. THE CHARACTERISTIC OF THE PRACTITIONER

The characteristic of the person who engages in this is that he should be of the highest capacity, with a mind weary of concrete phenomena.

Tsogyal, this can only be a person who possesses former training.

5. THE OBJECT FROM WHOM ONE RECEIVES

The object from whom you receive it should be one who has realized the single circle of dharmakaya and therefore remains in the state of the effortless great expanse.

Tsogyal, this can only be a master who has realized the meaning of the Great Perfection.

6. THE CEREMONY FOR RECEIVING

The ritual for receiving is the empowerment of awareness display.

Abandon your impure mundane physical activities as well as your pure virtuous actions. Remain like a person who has completed his deeds.

Abandon your impure unwholesome verbal utterances as well as your chanting and recitations and remain like a mute tasting sugar.

Abandon your impure samsaric thought activity as well as your

---

7. This refers to the two main aspects of Dzogchen practice: the primordial purity of *trekcho* and the spontaneous presence of *thogal*. These two practices must be learned through the oral instructions of a Dzogchen master.

pure nirvanic thought activity and remain like a person whose heart has been torn out.

By your master's mere indication you will thus perceive the primordial dharmakaya of your mind beyond the reach of words and description.

Tsogyal, this oral instruction of mine is a teaching of liberation simultaneous with understanding.

7. THE EFFECT OF TRAINING

The purpose of training in this is that without abandoning samsara it is liberated in itself, after which the disturbing emotions are spontaneously perfected as wisdoms. Thus it has the quality of bringing enlightenment in the present moment.

8. THE REASON FOR TRAINING

The reason for training in this way is that you must possess the nature free from bias and partiality.

9. THE SHORTCOMING OF NOT TRAINING

The danger of not training yourself is that you will fall into the partiality of philosophical schools and have the defect of being intrinsically fettered.

Tsogyal, if your practice falls into partiality it is not the Great Perfection.

10. THE POINTS TO BE OBSERVED

1. View as a mere convention that the root of all phenomena is contained within your own bodhicitta awareness, the primordial purity of nonarising.

2. See that this bodhicitta awareness is primordially enlightened since it does not possess any constructs such as a watcher or an object to be watched.

3. Recognize that whatever type of thought or fixation arises within the state of this awareness is primordially empty and luminous awareness itself.

4. Recognize that whatever outer appearances may arise do not

possess any identity whatsoever from the very moment they are experienced, and therefore do not transcend being the display of dharmata.

5. Experience the nonduality of objects and mind as the innate great bliss, free from accepting and rejecting, affirming or denying.

6. In particular, experience all disturbing emotions and suffering as the sacred path of enlightenment.

7. Realize that sentient beings, from the moment they are experienced, do not possess any true existence and therefore that samsara is the primordial purity of nonarising and does not have to be abandoned.

8. Realize that everything experienced as kayas and wisdoms is contained within your mind and therefore that buddhahood is beyond being accomplished.

Do this and you will become the successor of glorious Samantabhadra.

11. THE DIVIDING LINE BETWEEN LOSING AND POSSESSING AND THE METHOD OF REPAIRING WHEN DAMAGED

Here, there are no such efforts since you are primordially never separated from this throughout the three times.

EPILOGUE

Tsogyal, I have condensed the meaning of all the sutras, tantras, scriptures, and oral instructions into these outer, inner, and secret ways of arousing bodhicitta.

Put them into practice!
Bring them into the path!
Take them to heart!
Be in harmony with their meaning!
They are the root of the Mahayana teachings.

Thus he spoke.

This was the Mahayana training of bodhicitta entitled "The Teachings on Taking the Arousing of Bodhicitta as the Path." It was written down in Monkha Senge Dzong.[8]

Completed.
Treasure seal.
Concealment seal.
Entrustment seal.

ཨ་ལག་སརྨྱྲཿ མ་ས་ཧྲུཿ ཧ་ར་ཟ་ཡཿ

---

8. The last lines for the Lama Gongdue version, which had combined the teachings on refuge and bodhicitta into one reads:

These counsels on refuge and bodhicitta known as the foundation of precious gold are the basis of all Dharma practice. They are in harmony with all practitioners and are special instructions to be treasured by everyone.

According to the oral instructions given by Padmakara, the master of Uddiyana, for the sake of the beings of future generations, I, the princess of Kharchen, committed them to writing and concealed them as a precious treasure. May they meet with all worthy people in the future. SAMAYA.

ཨེ་ཚིག་བརྒྱུད་གྲུ་གུ། །ཞུས་ལན་ཟབ་མོའི་སྐོར་རྣམ་སོ།

The Ten Foundations of Secret Mantra
and Other Selected Teachings
The Cycle of Profound Advice through Questions and Answers

NAMO GURU.

The great master Padmakara was born from a lotus flower, untainted by a physical womb. He underwent various types of ascetic practices and finally attained the vidyadhara level of life mastery and there remains, having interrupted the river of birth and death.

He taught the 84,000 doors to the Dharma. He understands the tongues of the six classes of beings and of the eight classes of gods and demons. With his Brahma-like voice he brings benefit to all beings.

His mind possesses the realization of total omniscience. He has understood the nature that transcends arising and ceasing and he does not divide the nature of thigns with partiality.

As all required qualities arise from himself, he is the foundation and source of everything eminent. He is skilled in the means of taming all beings.

His activity invokes the minds of the sugatas and he controls the life force and heart of the eight classes of gods and demons.

Padmakara took birth on an island in the ocean and ruled the kingdom of Uddiyana. He practiced in the eight charnel grounds. Having undergone ascetic practices in India, through his compassion he came to Tibet. He fulfilled the wishes of the king of Tibet and established the kingdoms of India and Tibet in peace.

This kind master accepted as his spiritual consort me, Lady Tsogyal, the princess of Kharchen, from the time I was thirteen years of age. I was a mere girl who had faith, great compassion, an altruistic frame of mind, constancy, and sharp intelligence.

During the one hundred and eleven years[1] the master remained in Tibet, I served him and pleased him. Without exception, he bestowed upon me the entire extract of his oral instructions, the essence of his mind. During this time, I collected and committed to writing all the teachings that he gave and kept them concealed as precious treasures.[2]

TEN FOUNDATIONS OF TRAINING

The master said: When practicing the Dharma, you must train perfectly in the ten foundations of training.

The lady asked: What are these ten foundations of training?

The master said: You must resolve through the view, gaining understanding of all the teachings, like the garuda bird soaring in the skies.

You must find certainty through the conduct, without being intimidated by anything whatsoever, like an elephant entering the water.

You must practice through the samadhi, clearing away the darkness of ignorance, like lighting a lamp in a dark room.

You must accomplish the aim through the instructions, liberating all phenomena in your nature, like finding a wish-fulfilling jewel.

You must progress gradually through the empowerments, being free from the fear of falling into samsara, like a prince ascending the royal throne.

You must keep the basis through the samayas, not letting any of your actions be wasted, like fertile ground.

---

1. This way of counting must be in half years since most other sources tell that Padmakara stayed for exactly 55 years, naming all the places and the number of months each.

2. The number of teachings in each section in this chapter should not be taken too literally. During the centuries of copying these scriptures, some lines seem to have been lost.

You must liberate your being through learning, becoming adept in all aspects of the Dharma, like a noble steed freed from its chains.

You must compare all sources, understanding all the philosophical schools of the Dharma, like a bee seeking a hive.

You must condense them into a single point, understanding that all the numerous teachings are of one taste, like a trader adding together his profits.

You must reach eminence in knowledge, understanding clearly and distinctly the meaning of all the teachings, like arriving at the summit of Mount Sumeru.

The people of Tibet who desire to be learned without training themselves in these points are not learned in the essential meaning, but become practitioners with much sectarianism. This is due to the fault of not having become adept in these ten foundations of training.

TEN FAULTS

Master Padma said: You will possess the ten faults of being unsuccessful in Dharma practice when you have not become adept in the ten foundations of training.

The lady asked: What are those faults?

The master said: If you do not resolve through the view, you will have the fault that where you may fare lies uncertain.

If you do not find certainty through the conduct, you will have the fault of being unable to unite view and conduct.

If you do not know how to practice by means of samadhi, you will not perceive the nature of dharmata.

If you do not accomplish the aim through the oral instructions, you will not know how to practice.

If you do not progress gradually through the empowerments, you will not be suitable to practice the Dharma.

If you do not keep the basis through the samayas, you will plant the seeds for the hell realms.

If you do not liberate your being through learning, you will not taste the flavor of the Dharma.

If you do not compare all sources, you will not cut through the sectarianism of philosophical schools.

If you do not condense them into a single point, you will not comprehend the root of the Dharma.

If you do not reach eminence in knowledge, you will not perceive the nature of the Dharma.

The so-called spiritual teachers who have not trained themselves in Dharma practice do not comprehend that the Dharma is free from sectarian confines. They attack each other with great prejudice. Since all the vehicles are valid in themselves, do not get involved in bickering. Rest at ease.

TEN KEY POINTS

Master Padma said: When practicing the Dharma you must possess ten key points.

The lady asked: What are the ten key points?

The master said: You must possess the key point of faith free from fluctuation, like a river.

You must possess the key point of compassion free from enmity, like the sun.

You must possess the key point of generosity free from prejudice, like a spring of drinking water.

You must possess the key point of samaya free from flaws, like a crystal ball.

You must possess the key point of the view free from partiality, like space.

You must possess the key point of meditation free from being clarified or obscured, like the sky at dawn.

You must possess the key point of conduct free from adopting or avoiding, like dogs and pigs.

You must possess the key point of fruition free from abandonment or attainment, like arriving at an island of precious gold.

You must yearn for the Dharma like a starving person yearning for food or a thirsty man seeking water.

In any case, it seems that people only avoid practicing the Dharma as the main point, taking instead wealth as their focus. You cannot bring your wealth along at the time of death, so make sure not to go to the lower realms.

TEN TYPES OF SUPERFICIALITY

Master Padma said: There are many people who let their Dharma practice become superficial.

The lady asked: How is that?

The master said: It is superficial to chant the scriptures without having faith.

It is superficial to be altruistic without feeling compassion.

It is superficial to act generously without being free from stinginess.

It is superficial to be a tantrika who does not keep the samayas.

It is superficial to be a monk who does not keep the vows.

It is superficial to be noble without meditating.

It is superficial to have knowledge without practicing the Dharma.

It is superficial to engage oneself in a Dharma that does not possess the essence of practice.

It is superficial to teach others when one does not act in accordance with the Dharma oneself.

It is superficial to give advice that one does not follow oneself.

In any case, my ears are tired of listening to "learned" people whose Dharma practice does not tame their own minds but who simply let it add disturbing emotions; whatever they say is nothing but superficial talk.

TEN TYPES OF EXAGGERATION

Master Padma said: When practicing the Dharma, there are ten types of exaggeration.

The lady asked: What are they?

The master said: It is exaggeration to profess to know the Dharma without having listened to teachings.

It is exaggeration if you profess to have powers without having practiced sadhana.

It is exaggeration if you profess to receive the blessings without having devotion.

It is exaggeration if you profess to having attained buddhahood without having meditated.

It is exaggeration if you profess to have found a master without serving him.

It is exaggeration if you profess to be liberated through a teaching that has no lineage.

It is exaggeration if you profess to have realization without the oral instructions.

It is exaggeration if you profess that your being is liberated without having done any practice.

It is exaggeration if you profess to pratice without having diligence.

It is exaggeration if you profess to have auspicious circumstances without keeping the samayas.

In any case, people who wish to practice easily without undertaking hardship are nothing but braggarts and will have no success.

AVOIDING THE TEN FAULTS

Master Padma said: When practicing the Dharma, you must make sure not to fall into the ten faults.

The lady asked: What are these ten faults?

The master said: Although you may practice meditation, if it does not become a remedy against your disturbing emotions and thoughts, you have the fault of the oral instructions not being made effective.

Although you may have recognized your mind, if it does not liberate your consciousness free from partiality, you have the fault of not having met with the special instruction.

Although you may have strong devotion, if you do not receive the blessings, you have the fault of not having connected with an accomplished master.

Although you may exert yourself with great effort, if your practice does not progress, you have the fault of your mind not being fully purified.

If you feel tired when engaging in spiritual practice, you have the fault of not having recognized the natural state of awareness.

Although you practice, if your mind is still scattered, you have the fault of not having gained confidence in meditation.

If experience does not arise directly in your state of mind, you have the fault of having only strayed into shamatha.

If the strength of awareness does not arise in your being, you have the fault of not knowing how to take appearances as aids to the path.

If you find it difficult to cut through your attachment to disturbing emotions, you have the fault of not knowing how to take the five poisons as the path.

If you cannot cope with suffering and difficulties, you have the fault of not knowing how to turn your mind away from samsara.

In any case, when you claim to practice the Dharma while being full of faults within, is there any chance to ever have good circumstances?

TEN VIRTUOUS QUALITIES

Master Padma said: You need ten virtues as the sign of having practiced the Dharma.

The lady asked: What are these virtues?

The master said: If you can overcome discursive thinking, that is the sign of having recognized the natural state of awareness.

If the wisdom of mind essence manifests without partiality, that is the sign of the oral instructions having become effective.

If you perceive your master as a true buddha, that is the sign of having generated devotion to the master.

If you receive the blessings unimpededly, that is the sign that the lineage of siddhas is unbroken.

When applying awareness with effort, if you can change your state of mind unimpededly, that is the virtue of having trained the full power of awareness.

If you do not feel tired although you practice day and night, that is the virtue of having reached the key point of the prana-mind.

If there is no difference in clarity whether you pratice or not, that is the sign of having attained confidence in meditation.

If you can remind yourself of dharmata no matter what thought or appearance occurs to you, that is the sign of having taken appearances as an aid on the path.

If the zombie of disturbing emotions does not arise, or even if it does, if it is pacified immediately, that is the sign of spontaneously defeating the five poisons.

If you are invincible to suffering and difficulties, that is the virtue of having understood that impermanence is the characteristic of samsara.

In any case, virtues appear from within yourself when the Dharma dawns in your being. The Tibetan people who do not have faith, diligence, or intelligence will hardly have any virtues arising from within them.

TEN SIGNS

Master Padma said: When you take the Dharma to heart, there will be ten signs.

The lady asked: What are these ten signs?

The master said: When your grasping decreases, that is the sign of having expelled the evil spirit of fixation on concrete reality.

When your attachment grows less, that is the sign of being free from ambitious craving.

When your disturbing emotions decrease, that is the sign of the five poisons being pacified from within.

When your selfishness decreases, that is the sign of having expelled the evil spirit of ego-clinging.

When you are free from embarrassment and hold no reference point whatsoever, that is the sign that your deluded perception has collapsed.

When you are free from the concepts of meditator and meditation object and never lose sight of your innate nature, that is the sign that you have met the mother of dharmata.[3]

When any perception arises as unbiased individual experience, that is the sign of having reached the core of view and meditation.

When you have resolved samsara and nirvana as being indivisible, that is the sign that full realization has arisen within.

In short, when you have no clinging to even your own body, that is the sign of being totally free from attachment.

When you remain unharmed by suffering and difficulties, that is the sign of understanding appearances to be illusion.

---

3. This refers to the "mother luminosity" (ma'i 'od gsal), the ground luminosity of the natural state inherent as the enlightened essence of all sentient beings.

When you have only a minor degree of the eight worldly concerns, that is the sign of having recognized the nature of mind.

In any case, when your inner signs show outwardly it is like a tree that has sprouted leaves. When the outer signs are noticed by other people it is like fruit of the tree that has ripened and can be eaten.

There are many Dharma practitioners without even a single virtuous quality. People with realization are extremely rare, so it is essential to exert yourself in meditation practice.

TEN FACTS

Master Padma said: For all who can practice the Dharma there are ten facts.

The lady asked: What are they?

The master said: When the presence of the Buddha's teachings coincides with a person's attainment of a human body, it is a fact that he has gathered the accumulations in former lives.

When a person who has interest in the Dharma and a master who possesses the oral insructions meet, it is a fact that this is like a blind man finding a wish-fulfilling jewel.

When the attainment of the complete human body coincides with having faith and intelligence, it is a fact that your karmic continuity of former training has awakened.

When you are rich and at the same time met with beggars, it is a fact that the time has come to perfect generosity.

When the lake of misery overflows while you try to engage in spiritual practice, it is a fact that your evil karma and obscurations are being purified.

If you meet with uncaused enmity while trying to turn your mind to the Dharma, it is a fact that this is a guide to lead you on the path of patience.

When your understanding of the impermanence of conditioned things and your possession of perfect faith coincide with receiving the profound instructions, it is a fact that the time has come to turn your mind away from the life of a worldly person.

When your fear of dying coincides with the death of another

person, it is a fact that the time has come for exceptional faith to arise.

In any case, if you first try to accomplish worldly pursuits and plan to engage in Dharma practice later on, it is amazing if you will find the chance to do so! Thus only few are liberated from samsara.

SEVEN CORRUPTIONS

Master Padma said: When practicing the Dharma there are seven types of corruption.

The lady asked: What are they?

The master said: If your faith is small while your intelligence is great, you become corrupted by considering yourself a teacher.

If you have many listeners while your self-regard is high, you become corrupted by considering yourself a spiritual friend.

If you assume superior qualities while not having taken the Dharma to heart, you become corrupted by considering yourself a leader.

If you give oral instructions while not practicing them yourself, you become corrupted by being an insensitive "Dharma expert."

If you are fond of senseless babble while lacking the Dharma in your heart, you become corrupted by being a craving charlatan yogi.

If you have little learning while lacking the oral instructions, you become corrupted by being a commoner though your faith may be great.

A genuine practitioner who acts in accordance with the true teachings should liberate his being with intelligence, tame his mind with faith, cut misconceptions with listening to teachings, cast away social concerns, mingle his mind with the Dharma, perfect his knowledge with learning and reflecting, resolve his mind with the oral instructions, and gain final certainty through the view and meditation. That, however, is difficult.

THE DANGER OF MISTAKES

Master Padma said: There can be many types of mistakes for people who have entered the gate of the Dharma. Be careful!

The lady asked: What are they?

The master said: It is possible to mistake a teacher who has studied intelligently for a spiritual friend whose being is liberated through learning and reflection.

It is possible to mistake an insensitive "Dharma-expert," who has not practiced himself, for someone who has gained experience through personal practice.

It is possible to mistake a deceitful hypocrite for a noble being who has tamed his mind through Dharma practice.

It is possible to mistake empty words of hollow eloquence for the realization of someone possessing the oral instructions.

It is possible to mistake a braggart spouting the Dharma for the devotion to Dharma practice of a faithful person.

In any case, you must make sure to mingle your mind with the Dharma. People who practice the Dharma of lip service, claiming to be practitioners while keeping the Dharma as something apart from themselves, will have no success in Dharma pratice.

FOUR DHARMAS

Master Padma said: You must make sure your Dharma practice becomes the real Dharma. You must make sure your Dharma becomes the real path. You must make sure your path can clarify confusion. You must make sure your confusion dawns as wisdom.

The lady asked: What does that mean?

The master said: When you have understanding free from accepting and rejecting after knowing how to condense all the teachings into a single vehicle, then your Dharma practice becomes the real Dharma.

When the three vipashyana states of bliss, clarity, and nonthought dawn, they are dharmakaya itself.

In any case, there are many people who fix their minds on an inert state of shamatha. Through that they will be reborn either in the dhyana realms of the gods or, even if they do not incarnate, they will still be unable to benefit beings.

THE VOWS

Master Padma said: Taking refuge and keeping vows are the root of Dharma practice.

The lady asked: At what time do the refuge vow and the other vows arise in one's being?

The master said: The refuge vow arises the moment you feel fear of the lower realms and have faith in the Three Jewels.

The vow of a lay person arises the moment you have trust in the cause and result of karmic actions.

The vow of a novice arises the moment your mind has turned away from samsara.

The vow of a fully ordained person arises the moment your mind has turned away from all wrongdoing.

The bodhicitta vow of aspiration arises the moment you out of compassion see yourself as equal to others.

The bodhicitta of application arises the moment you regard others as more important than yourself.

When in any practice you do you possess refuge and bodhicitta, and have unified the stages of development and completion, and means and knowledge, then your Dharma becomes the real path.

When you combine the path with the view, meditation, action, and fruition, then your path clarifies confusion.

When you exert yourself in practice having fully resolved the view and meditation, then your confusion can dawn as wisdom.

In any case, no matter what practice you do, failing to unify development and completion, view and conduct, and means and knowledge will be like trying to walk on just one leg.

AVOIDING THE DHYANA REALMS

Master Padma said: When practicing the Dharma, it is important to avoid letting your practice turn into a lower vehicle.

The lady asked: What does that mean?

The master said: It is crucial to avoid clinging to the three shamatha states of bliss, clarity, and nonthought. If you cling to them, you cannot escape becoming a shravaka or pratyekabuddha.

The people of Tibet regard the practice of taking refuge as the lowest teaching. The monastics have no discipline. Those who claim to practice Mahayana have no bodhicitta. The tantrikas do not keep their samayas. The yogis have no true meditation.

It will be difficult to have any siddhas here in Tibet.

THE SAMAYAS OF BODY, SPEECH, AND MIND

Master Padma said: When practicing the Dharma you must keep the samayas, but that is difficult.

The lady asked: How should one keep the samayas?

The master said: When perceiving your master as a buddha in person you possess the samaya of enlightened body.

When perceiving his words and teachings as the wish-fulfilling jewel you possess the samaya of enlightened speech.

When perceiving his oral instructions as nectar you possess the samaya of enlightened mind.

When you cease to accept or reject the yidam you possess the samaya of body.

When you have no doubt about the Secret Mantra you possess the samaya of speech.

When you understand the meaning of the natural state of mind-essence you possess the samaya of mind.

In any case, the samayas are pure when your mind is pure.

FIFTEEN ADVERSE CIRCUMSTANCES

Master Padma said: When practicing the Dharma there can be fifteen adverse circumstances that you must give up.

The lady asked: What are they?

The master said: Idle gossip, banter, and frivolity are the three obstacles to meditation, so give them up.

Relatives, friends, and disciples are the three diversions of Dharma practice, so give them up.

Material things, business, and enjoyments are the three distractions for Dharma practice, so give them up.

Gain, fame, and honor are the three fetter-poles of Dharma practice, so give them up.

Sleep, indolence, and laziness are the three arch-enemies of Dharma practice, so give them up.

In any case, the most dangerous is to be dissuaded when practicing the Dharma.

FIFTEEN CONDUCIVE CIRCUMSTANCES

Master Padma said: When practicing the Dharma, you should possess fifteen conducive circumstances.

The lady asked: What are they?

The master said: Learning, reflecting, and meditating are the basic frameworks of Dharma practice.

Diligence, faith, and trust are the three life-poles of Dharma practice.

Knowledge, discipline, and goodness are the three characters of Dharma practice.

Nonattachment, nonclinging, and nonfixation are the three harmonious factors for Dharma practice.

In any case, there is not even one Dharma practitioner here who possesses even three of these conditions. It is difficult to be in accordance with the main principles of the Dharma.

TWENTY-ONE TYPES OF FUTILITY

Master Padma said: When practicing the Dharma, there are twenty-one types of futility.

The lady asked: What are they?

The master said: It is futile to generate bodhicitta if you have not given up causing harm to sentient beings.

It is futile to receive empowerments if you do not keep the samayas.

It is futile to learn many teachings if they do not benefit your own mind.

It is futile to perform roots of virtue if they are mixed with evil deeds.

It is futile to follow a master if you always engage in misdeeds.

It is futile to become a teacher who gives up Dharma practice and commits misdeeds.

It is futile to carry out a task that promotes the eight worldly concerns.

It is futile to follow a teacher who is always hostile to sentient beings, who are your own parents.

It is futile to claim that you have fear of the hells if you constantly engage in evil deeds.

It is futile to perform acts of generosity if you do not embrace them by bodhicitta and have no faith.

It is futile to take vows if you lack the determination to keep them.

It is futile to practice patience if you do not embrace your anger by the right remedy.

It is futile to practice meditation if your mind is always involved in either dullness or agitation.

It is futile to exert yourself with a diligence that does not aim toward the path of enlightenment.

It is futile to develop perverted knowledge that increases envy and the other five poisons.

It is futile to practice a Mahayana teaching that lacks the path of compassion.

It is futile to practice a meditation state that lacks understanding of the nature of your mind.

It is futile to receive oral instructions if you do not put them into practice.

It is futile to act for the benefit of beings without having embraced those acts with bodhicitta.

In any case, although these things are futile and although there is no need for many such activities, childish people will not listen.

FOUR TYPES OF NONRETURN

Master Padma said: When practicing the Dharma, you must possess the four types of nonreturn.

The lady asked: What are they?

The master said: By remembering death you will not fall back into concerns for this life.

By cultivating the results of the ten virtuous actions you will not fall back into the three lower realms.

By cultivating loving-kindness you will not fall back into the lower vehicles.

By meditating on emptiness you will not fall back into samsara.

In any case, when practicing the Dharma you need to turn your mind away form the concerns of this life.

FOUR THINGS THAT WILL NOT HAPPEN

Master Padma said: When practicing the Dharma, there are four things that should not happen. They should therefore be abandoned.

The lady asked: What are they?

The master said: If you do not remember death, you will find no time to practice the Dharma.

If due to lacking trust in the law of karma you do not give up unvirtuous actions, you will find no chance to achieve the higher realms and liberation.

If you do not fear the miseries of samsara and have no renunciation, you will have no success in the practices for attaining liberation.

If you desire to attain emancipation and liberation for yourself alone without arousing the intent of attaining enlightenment for the sake of others, you will have no chance of attaining complete buddhahood.

In general, if you do not turn away from aims limited to this lifetime, you will have no success in Dharma practice whatsoever. There are not even a few who have given up worldly concerns.

TAKING ADVANTAGE

Master Padma said: When practicing the Dharma, you must take advantage of four futile things.

The lady asked: What are they?

The master said: In order to take advantage of the body that is futile, observe your discipline purely.

In order to take advantage of possessions that are futile, be generous while keeping bodhicitta in mind.

In order to take advantage of good conditions that are futile, gather the accumulation of merit as the cause and the accumulation of wisdom as the result.

In order to take advantage of learning that is futile, exert yourself in meaningful practice.

Unless you know how to take advantage in these ways, whatever you do is nothing but worldly activity.

FIVE UNMISTAKEN THINGS

Master Padma said: When practicing the Dharma, you must possess the five unmistaken things.

The lady asked: What are they?

The master said: You must unmistakenly observe the precepts and vows you have taken.

You must always be unmistaken about the practice of love, compassion, and bodhicitta.

When contemplating the law of cause and effect of karmic actions, you must unmistakenly shun even the tiniest misdeed.

When meditating on your master as a buddha you must unmistakenly always visualize him above the crown of your head.

In any case, you must be unmistaken when contemplating that all phenomena are emptiness.

PRACTICING THE SIX PARAMITAS

Master Padma said: When practicing the Dharma, you must practice by means of the six paramitas.

The lady asked: How does one practice them?

The master said: When you do not harbor any stinginess or prejudice whatsoever in your mind, that is the paramita of generosity.

When you can skillfully relinquish your disturbing emotions, that is the paramita of discipline.

When you are totally free from anger and resentment, that is the paramita of patience.

When you are neither lazy nor indolent, that is the paramita of diligence.

When you are free from distraction and attachment to the taste of meditation, that is the paramita of concentration.

When you are utterly free from constructed concepts, that is the paramita of discriminating knowledge.

THREE KINDS OF PURSUITS

The master said: When practicing the Dharma, there are three kinds of pursuits.

The lady asked: What are they?

The master said: The inferior person pursues activities only for the sake of future lives, without putting effort into other activities. Thus, there is no way he will avoid attaining the higher realms.

The mediocre person, feeling weary of the whole of samsara, pursues only virtuous activities. Thus, there is no way he will avoid attaining liberation.

The superior person pursues only the practice of bodhicitta for the sake of all sentient beings. Thus, there is no way he will avoid attaining complete enlightenment.

In general, all the aims that people pursue from the break of dawn to the close of day are merely for the sake of pleasure in this lifetime. Disturbed by negative emotions in this life, there is no way they can avoid going to the lower realms in following lives.

FIVE TRUE WAYS OF MOURNING

Master Padma said: People who practice the Dharma feel great sorrow at the death of their own relatives. That is not the correct way. When practicing the Dharma there are five things to mourn.

The lady asked: What are they?

The master said: When separated from an eminent master, you should mourn by making funeral offerings.

When separated from a good Dharma friend, you should mourn by gathering the accumulations.

When you go against your master, you should mourn by admitting it remorsefully.

When you damage or break your vows, you should mourn by repairing and purifying them.

When you have been unable to practice for a long time, you should mourn by following a master.

When your mind strays into the eight worldly concerns, you should mourn by feeling deep renunciation.

In any case, people who do not understand that conditioned things are impermanent will never exhaust or clear away their sorrow.

FOUR WAYS OF FARMING

Master Padma said: When practicing the Dharma, you must possess the four ways of farming.

The lady asked: What are they?

The master said: You must till the rugged soil of your mind with the solid faith of trust.

You must apply the soft manure of changing your attitude with the practice of meditation.

You must sow the good seeds of virtuous roots by embracing them with bodhicitta.

You must completely destroy the five poisons and all discursive thinking by letting the plowman of great diligence fasten the plowshare of wisdom to the plow oxen of unified means and knowledge.

If you do like that, it is impossible to avoid the sprouts of enlightenment growing into the fruition of buddhahood.

In any case, there are too many who cannot do the farming of liberation, while never feeling tired of worldy farming. Poor sentient beings!

EIGHT KINDS OF SILENCE

The master said: When practicing the Dharma, you need to keep eight kinds of silence.

The lady asked: What are they?

The master said: To keep the silence of body, stay in retreat places without falling into any extreme. Through this you will turn away from passion and aggression.

To keep the silence of speech, remain in the manner of a mute. Through this you will not be distracted from spiritual practice by gossiping with others.

To keep the silence of mind, do not let yourself be governed by discursive thoughts and distractions. This will allow you to abide in the innate nature of dharmakaya beyond thoughts.

To keep the silence of sense pleasures, abandon the concepts of pure and impure food. This will make living simple and will cause the dakinis to gather.

To keep the silence of oral instructions, do not give them to unsuitable people. This will enable you to receive the blessings of the lineage.

To keep the silence of conduct, act spontaneously and without hypocrisy. This will enable progress and prevent your mind from collecting obscurations.

To keep the silence of experience, be free from attachment or fascination with your experiences and do not relate them to others. This will enable you to attain the siddhi of mahamudra within this lifetime.

To keep the silence of realization, be free from ambition and rest without falling into any extreme. This will enable you to be liberated instantly in the moment of realization.

In general, people who cannot practice for even the duration of a meal, who are unable to remain silent until the session of recitation is completed, and who cannot keep their chattering mouths shut, will not have even the slightest success in keeping silence.

THE SEDUCTIONS OF MARA

Master Padma said: Dharma practitioners do not notice when they have been deceived by Mara.

The lady asked: What does that mean?

The master said: Powerful people are deceived by the Mara of pride and conceit.

Dignitaries are deceived by the Mara of eloquence and delusion.

Commoners are deceived by the Mara of ignorance and stupidity.

Rich people are deceived by the Mara of busy aims and the promotion of their wealth.

Dharma practitioners are deceived by the Mara of increasing their material possessions.

They are deceived by the Mara of bringing up children, their karmic creditors.

They are deceived by the Mara of respectful disciples.

They are deceived by the Mara of loving servants and attendants.

They are deceived by the Mara of hated enemies.

They are deceived by the Mara of affectionate words from relatives.

They are deceived by the Mara of beautiful physical ornaments.

They are deceived by the Mara of gentle voices and sweet-sounding words.

They are deceived by the Mara of their own attachment.

They are deceived by the Mara of beauty and yearning for affection.

All your effort in deluded actions is the seduction of Mara.

The five poisons inherent in yourself are the Mara of your mind.

The six sense objects remaining as habitual tendencies are the Mara of outer things.

Clinging to the taste of samadhi is the Mara of inner phenomena.

Hoping for fruition in Dzogchen is the Mara of the view.

All superior qualities are also Mara.

All ignorance and delusion are also Mara.

The greatest Mara is therefore ego-clinging.

It does not exist anywhere else but within yourself. You must kill this demon from within. If you do that, he will not come from outside.

There are only too many people who do not recognize this Mara.

FOUR BASIC QUALITIES

Master Padma said: When practicing the Dharma, you must possess four basic qualities.

The lady asked: What are they?

The master said: The person who has great compassion will possess the mind of enlightenment.

The person who is free from hypocrisy will be able to keep the precepts.

The person who is without deceit has pure samayas.

The person who is free from affectation will have no shame and no fair-weather friendship.

In any case, if you have great faith you will also have success in Dharma practice and if you are decisive you will be able to keep your vows. In order to practice the Dharma you must be careful; be as firm as a bone in the core of your heart.

CUTTING THE FIVE POISONS AT THEIR ROOT

Master Padma said: When practicing the Dharma, you must cut the five poisons at their root.

The lady asked: What does that mean?

The master said: The person with strong anger has the most suffering.

The person with great stupidity is like a beast and cannot understand the Dharma.

The person with vast pride cannot assimilate virtues and has many enemies.

The person with strong desire cannot keep the vows and will be slandered a lot.

The person with great envy has strong ambitions and delights in intrigue.

Do not chase after these five poisons; you kill them from within by freeing them the moment they arise.

People who unrestrainedly engage in the five poisons are creating their own misery.

TAMING ONE'S MIND

Master Padma said: When practicing the Dharma, you must first tame your own mind.

The lady asked: What does that mean?

The master said: You must extinguish the scorching flames of anger with the water of loving-kindness.

You must cross the river of desire on the bridge of powerful remedies.

You must light the torch of discriminating knowledge in the darkness of stupidity.

You must crumble the mountain of pride to the ground with the pestle of diligence.

You must overcome the storm of envy by wearing the warm garment of patience.

In any case, these five poisons, your old archenemies, will ruin your being in the three realms of samsara if you uninhibitedly indulge in them. Do not let them run wild. There is a danger in that.

THE FIVE SIGNS OF SEEING

Master Padma said: When practicing the Dharma, you must possess the five signs of seeing.

The lady asked: What are they?

The master said: You must see the immaterial nature of mind beyond the words of the sacred Dharma.

You must see that these present appearances are self-liberated when free from fixation.

You must see that whichever experience may arise is immaterial great bliss.

With respect and devotion, you must see your master as a buddha in person.

In any case, when practicing the Dharma you must see everything free from attachment.

THE FIVE ATTAINMENTS

Master Padma said: When practicing the Dharma, you must possess the five types of attainment.

The lady asked: What are they?

The master said: Without abandoning your master's oral instructions by being lazy, you must possess the actual application of practice.

You must possess the benefit of self by having engaged in practice yourself.

You must possess the ability of guiding disciples for the benefit of others by possessing the transmission of blessings.

You must possess the attainment of unfabricated naturalness by liberating appearances into the dharmata.

You must possess the attainment of your mind being the buddha by recognizing your natural face.

The Tibetan practitioners of the present day who do not possess even one of these will not accomplish even one of their wishes.

THE FIVE TYPES OF GREATNESS

Master Padma said: When practicing the Dharma, you must possess the five types of greatness.

The lady asked: What are they?

The master said: You must have a master with the greatness of the oral instructions.

These oral instructions must also be endowed with the greatness of the profound path of skillful means.

You yourself must have the greatness of fortitude in undertaking hardship.

You must possess the greatness of aspiration toward Dharma practice.

You must have greatness of determination in practicing.

Unless you possess these five when trying to be liberated from samsara you will not be successful.

FIVE KINDS OF MASTERY

Master Padma said: When practicing the Dharma, you must possess five types of mastery.

The lady asked: What are they?

The master said: By gaining natural mastery over the Dharma, you must possess the "knowing one that frees all."

By gaining realization of dharmata, you must let the nonarising dawn within your being.

By gaining natural mastery over samaya, you must possess flawlessness of mind.

By gaining mastery over the pranas through exertion, you must be able to undertake hardship.

By gaining mastery over the oral instructions, you must be able to teach people according to their own dispositions.

FIVE SUPERFLUOUS THINGS

Master Padma said: When practicing the Dharma, there are five things that are superfluous.

The lady asked: What are they?

The master said: It is superfluous to generate devotion while you have no renunciation for samsara.

It is superfluous to contemplate emptiness while you have not turned away from clinging to materiality.

It is superfluous to practice meditation while you have not turned away from craving.

It is superfluous to expound an oral instruction while you have not turned away from attachment and aggression.

It is superfluous to give well-sounding advice that does not accord with the expedient meaning.[4]

FIVE NECESSARY THINGS

Master Padma said: When practicing the Dharma, there are five necessary things.

The lady asked: What are they?

The master said: It is necessary to be accepted by noble beings so that you can obtain the essence of the oral instructions.

It is necessary to have deep and unceasing devotion to your master so that you can naturally receive the blessings.

It is necessary to gather a particular degree of the accumulations so that your mind can be pliant.

It is necessary that your mind be pliant so that samadhi can dawn in your being.

---

4. "Expedient meaning" refers to the relative truth.

It is necessary that samadhi dawn in your being so that you quickly attain the omniscient state of buddhahood.

FIVE LIES

Master Padma said: When claiming to be a practitioner, there are five things that become a lie.

The lady asked: What are they?

The master said: It is a lie to say that you fear for the future rebirth while being totally enamored of this life.

It is a lie to say that you are taking refuge while committing actions with no dread of the three lower realms.

It is a lie to say that you are a meditator while your mind has not turned away from craving.

It is a lie to say that you have understood the view while not knowing about cause and effect.

It is a lie to say that you are a buddha while not having crossed the abyss of samsaric existence.

There are many people who claim to be Dharma practitioners and lie to both others and themselves. At the time of passing away, all the lies will be on themselves.

FIVE WORDS OF CERTAINTY

The master said: When practicing the Dharma, one needs to possess the instruction with five words of certainty.

The lady asked: What are they?

The master said: Without meditating, it is certain that experience and realization will not occur.

If means and knowledge become separated in Mahayana practice, it is certain that you will fall down to the shravaka level.

If you do not know how to unite view and conduct, it is certain that you will take an errant path.

Without true realization of mind essence, it is certain that there exist both virtuous and evil actions.

Without realizing your own mind, it is certain that you will not attain buddhahood.

FIVE FUTILE THINGS

The master said: When practicing the Dharma, there are five things that are futile. Avoid them!

The lady asked: What are they?

The master said: It is futile to follow a master who does not possess the essence of the instructions.

It is futile to give teachings to a disciple who does not uphold his commitments.

It is futile to know teachings that you do not utilize and put into practice.

It is futile to apply meditations that do not improve your mind.

It is futile to engage in shallow teachings of mere talk that do not help yourself.

In general, there are many people who practice what is futile. Because of ignorance they do not know the difference.

SIX NOBLE QUALITIES

Master Padma said: When practicing the Dharma, you must possess six noble qualities.

The lady asked: What are they?

The master said: In order to master the view you must understand that everything is mind.

In order to be free from hypocrisy in your discipline you must clear your mind of defilements.

In order to practice generosity without prejudice you must be free from expecting gratitude or reward.

In order to be able to face difficulties with patience you must be free from anger toward enemies.

In order to train your mind through learning and reflection you must be able to take the five poisons and painful experiences as the path.

In order to meditate you must be able to avoid being carried away by the "Mara of meritorious action."[5]

---

5. The seduction to aim one's spiritual practice toward selfish ends; virtuous deeds that are not embraced by renunciation or bodhicitta.

However, these practitioners do not act in harmony with the Dharma.

FOUR DEFECTS

Master Padma said: When practicing the Dharma, you must give up four kinds of defects.

The lady asked: What are they?

The master said: It is not sufficient to practice at lesiure; your practice must be unceasing like the flow of a river.

It is not sufficient to reach the experience of seeing spirits; you must liberate your mind through Dharma practice.

It is not sufficient to be hypocritical in your conduct; it must be natural and spontaneous.

It is not sufficient to show respect and make promises; you must actually serve at the feet of a master.

In any case, the practitioners here are not free from these four defects; at the time of death they will die as ordinary people and reap the consequences.

PRETENTIOUSNESS

Master Padma said: These Dharma practitioners are braggarts with too high self-esteem; they are even worse than ordinary people.

The lady asked: What does that mean?

The master said: They claim to practice the Dharma and to follow a master. They pretend to be teachers or to have many monks. They claim to manage a monastery and to make exquisite offerings. They pretend to exert themselves in spiritual practice and to have higher perceptions. They claim to stay in strict retreat and possess the highest teachings. To try to fool others by hypocritical deeds while failing to divest oneself from worldly conceit will only be cause for regret at the time of death!

FOURTEEN THINGS TO LEAVE BEHIND

Master Padma said: If you want to practice the Dharma from the core of your heart, there are fourteen things that you must leave behind.

The lady asked: What are they?

The master said: Be a child of the wild deer and live in secluded mountain dwellings.

Eat the food of fasting, practice the asceticism of "extracting essences."[6]

Do not roam among the upper class in the capital, keep a low profile in your conduct.

Act in a way that pleases your enemies and cut all ties to your homeland.

Dress in castaway clothing and be humble.

Abandon attachment to relatives and friendships and sever all your ties.

Try to emulate the buddhas and engage in practice.

Entrust your heart to the oral instructions and apply them in practice.

Take your yidam as the innermost essence and recite its mantra.

Regard misdeeds as being the most vile and give them up.

Be generous toward your master and offer him whatever you can.

Leave samsara behind and give rise to weariness.

Offer your victory to others and do not compete with the powerful.

Take defeat yourself and expose your own faults.

By acting in this way your Dharma practice will progress as the true Dharma and you will turn away from samsara.

THREE DISEASES TO ABANDON

Master Padma said: When practicing the Dharma, there are three diseases you must abandon.

The lady asked: What are they?

The master said: Unless you abandon your homeland, the disease of the land, you will be caught in the prison of the five poisons and fall into the lower realms.

Unless you abandon the clinging to owning house and property,

---

6. Skt. *rasayana*, a yogic practice of living off the essences of medicinal plants, minerals, and the energy of the five elements.

the disease of dwelling place, you will be caught in the dungeon of grasping and ego-clinging and not be able to cut through the Mara of attachment.

Unless you abandon offspring and family, the disease of relatives, you will be caught in the muddy swamp of samsara and find no chance for liberation.

It requires indeed great tolerance to live in the house of samsara without having abandoned these three diseases and yet still not notice being tormented by the sickness of the three poisons.

THE WAY TO BE LIBERATED FROM SAMSARA

Master Padma said: When practicing the Dharma, there are ways to be liberated from samsara.

The lady asked: What should we do?

The master said: If you wish to give rise to extraordinary devotion, observe the guru's outer and inner virtues.

If you wish to act in harmony with everyone, do not falter in your efforts to benefit others.

If you wish to realize the mind of the guru, put his oral instructions into practice.

If you wish to attain the siddhis swiftly, never fail to keep your samayas.

If you wish to be freed from the four floods of birth, old age, sickness, and death, be incessant in resolving the nonarising all-ground.[7]

If you wish to be without obstacles in practice, cast worldly distractions behind you.

If you wish to effortlessly accomplish the benefit of others, train your mind in the bodhicitta of immeasurable love and compassion.

If you dread going to the three lower realms in your next life, give up the ten unvirtuous actions in this lifetime.

If you wish to have happiness in both this and future lifetimes, exert yourself in the ten virtuous actions.

---

7. In this case, the "all-ground" (*kun gzhi, alaya*) is synonymous with dharmakaya.

If you wish to engage your mind in the Dharma, persevere in your practice during hardship and misery.

If you wish to turn away from samsara, search for unexcelled enlightenment within your own mind.

If you wish to achieve the fruition of the three kayas, exert yourself in gathering the two accumulations.

If you practice in this way, you will find happiness. People who have not turned their minds away from samsara have no happiness.

PRACTICING THE DHARMA WITH SINCERITY

Master Padma said: If you want to practice the Dharma from the core of your heart, there is a way.

The lady asked: What is that?

When engaging yourself in sadhana, be free from attachment and anger.

When you study in the correct way, wear the armor of patience.

When dwelling in secluded places, do not be attached to food or wealth.

If you yearn for the Dharma practice that leads to attainment, follow a master who has gained accomplishment.

If you have met with a sublime teacher, do not turn against him but try your best to please him.

When you feel doubt about the Dharma, ask your master for advice.

When your relatives turn against you, cut off your ties of attachment.

Cast away being distracted by obstacles or ghosts.

Practice immediately without procrastination.

Do not yearn for company but remain in solitude.

Friends and possessions, relatives and material things, are all illusory, so give them up.

Attachment and aggression will well up if you keep the company of other people.

Live alone and engage in spiritual practice.

Many diversions will only interrupt your practice, so give them up.

In any case, people who are unable to engage in spiritual practice will find no true happiness.

KEEPING THE SAMAYAS

Master Padma said: When practicing the Dharma, you must keep the samayas. It seems that people do nothing but violate their samayas because they are unable to undertake hardship.

The lady asked: What does that mean?

The master said: There are violators who keep their master a secret, claim to be learned, and only promote their own greatness.

There are violators who intend to make an offering to their master and then change their minds, keeping the offering deceitfully as a part of their own wealth.

There are violators who cheat and deceive both their master and Dharma friends.

There are violators who disparage their kind master and then brag about their own fame.

There are violators who project their own faults onto their master and still pretend to have pure samayas.

There are violators who think they can judge the unjudgable life-example of their master.

There are violators who proclaim their master's virtues to others but in the end aim at rivaling him.

There are many stubborn people who claim to have knowledge without having listened to teachings, who claim to be ripened without having received empowerment and who claim to possess the oral instructions when they have not received them. Thus there are only a few who receive blessings and powers.

CONSTANT FAITH

Master Padma said: When practicing the Dharma, constant faith is alone of great importance. There are ten causes for giving rise to faith.

The lady asked: What are they?

The master said: Recognize that your present activities, gain, and fame contain no happiness.

Trust in the karmic results of both virtuous actions and misdeeds.

Feel weariness while remembering that you will die.

Understand that wealth and possessions, children, spouse, and relatives are unimportant since they will not accompany you at the time of death.

Understand that you have no power to choose your environment in the next life, since it is uncertain where one will take rebirth.

Recognize that without practicing the Dharma after having obtained a complete human body you will leave this life empty-handed.

Recognize that no matter where you may be reborn among the six realms of samsara you are never beyond suffering.

Hear about the superior qualities of the Three Jewels.

Perceive the special actions of a sacred master as being good qualities.

Keep company with good Dharma friends who abide by what is virtuous.

The person who remembers or give rise to these things will turn away from samsara. But isn't it difficult to give rise to even one of them?

THIRTEEN RENUNCIATIONS

Master Padma said: If you want to practice the Dharma from the core of your heart, you must possess the thirteen types of renunciation.

The lady asked: What are they?

The master said: If you do not renounce your homeland you cannot defeat the Mara of pride.

If you do not give up the activities of a householder you will not find the time to practice the Dharma.

If you do not embrace the Dharma when you feel faith, you will not bring an end to karma.

While you have no faith yourself, give up disparaging others.

If you cannot abandon your own belongings, you will not be able to cut through worldly affairs.

If you do not keep your distance from relatives, you will not break the flow of attachment and anger.

If you do not practice the Dharma right now, it is not sure where you will be reborn in the following life.

If you aspire to do something in the future instead of doing it right now while you have the opportunity, it is not sure that it will ever happen.

Do not fool yourself; cut your ambitions and practice the sacred Dharma.

Give up relatives and friends, lovers and belongings. If you do so right now, it will be most significant.

Do not promote some unvirtuous social position that you definitely can't take along; promote virtuous actions that are definitely necessary.

Do not make preparations for tomorrow that may or may not be necessary; engage instead in preparing for death through spiritual practice. That is definitely necessary.

If you exert yourself in Dharma practice, you do not have to worry about food and clothing; they will be obtained automatically. I have never heard about or seen anyone who starved to death while practicing the Dharma.

THIRTEEN IMPORTANT THINGS

The master said: To pracatice the Dharma sincerely, you must practice these thirteen imporant actions.

The lady asked: What are they?

The master said: It is important to attend a master who possesses good qualities.

It is important to follow for a long time a master who possesses the oral instructions.

It is important to have steadfast devotion to the sublime Three Jewels.

It is important to shun even the most subtle nonvirtue and evil deed.

It is important to reflect on impermanence three times during the day and three times at night.

It is important to be diligent in practicing the virtuous Dharma.

It is important to cultivate love and compassion for sentient beings at all times.

It is important to skillfully cast away attachment to appearances and material things.

It is important to gain certainty in the unerring oral instructions.

It is important to keep the samayas and vows in the proper manner.

It is important to become clear about your own mind.

It is important not to divulge the secret instructions to unsuitable persons.

When practicing, it is important to exert yourself and stay in secluded places.

When you practice these, your Dharma practice will be successful.

THE WAY OF THE DHARMA

Master Padma said: If you want to practice the Dharma, here is the way.

The lady asked: What should one do?

The master said: If you wish to perceive the meaning of dharmata, you must follow a master.

If you desire to be liberated from samsara, you must abandon the life of a householder.

If you realize that you have to die, you must practice the Dharma.

If you wish to practice nonduality, you must give up activities.

If you wish to perfect good qualities, you must accomplish the practices.

If you desire to cast away misery, you must abandon followers and attendants.

If you desire to gain experience, you must frequent mountain retreats.

If you want to be free from attachment, you must give up your homeland.

If you wish to watch a spectacle, you must look into the luminous mirror of your mind.

If you wish to become accomplished, you must venerate the guru, the yidam, and the dakini above your head.

There seems to be no one who practices the teachings of attaining liberation.

PERSEVERANCE

Master Padma said: When practicing the Dharma from your heart, you most possess perseverance.

The lady asked: What does that mean?

Friends and offspring, food and wealth, are all delusions, so give them up.

Diversions, honor, and positive conditions are all severe obstacles, so give them up.

Companionship, relatives, and attendants are all roots of samsara and causes for attachment and anger, so give them up.

The years and months, the days and moments, are all what shorten the time left before the moment of death, so practice quickly.

People without perseverance and a true purpose regard their relatives, food, wealth, and offspring as being exceptional. They regard distractions as positive conditions. They regard companionship as pleasant. Without noticing the passing of years, months, and days, they count the length of their life. At the time of death, they will have to be their own guides.

THE DIFFICULTY OF PRACTICING THE DHARMA

Master Padma said: It is indeed difficult to practice the Dharma.

The lady asked: What does that mean?

The master said: There is the danger of holding wrong views.

The meditation is mistaken by mental fabrication.

The worst enemy is broken samayas.

The conduct is deluded by unvirtuous actions of body, speech, and mind.

The teachings are destroyed by too much ambition.

The Dharma wanes by aiming to obtain wealth.

The vows are spoiled by criticizing others.

The path is mistaken by clinging to suffering as being real.

Modesty is lost by craving desirable things.

The goal is mistaken by all the gain and fame of this life.

Teachers without Dharma practice are embarrassing and such meditators are depressing.

WAYS TO FEEL AT EASE

The master said: There are ways to feel at ease if you know how.

The lady said: Please explain that!

The master said: When free from dualistic fixation, the view is easy.

When free from drowsiness, agitation, and distraction, meditation is easy.

When attachment is purified like space, the conduct is easy.

When the stains of your mind are purified, experience is easy.

When your mind is free from distress, your own dwelling place feels easy.

When partiality is purified, compassion is easy.

When fixation is purified from within, generosity is easy.

When knowing food and wealth to be illusory, enjoyment is easy.

When you do not have an arrogant profile, your daily activities are easy.

When you do not lead the life of a householder putting up with misery, livelihood is easy.

When you do not compete for noble qualities, companionship is easy.

When free from childish behavior and ego-clinging, one is at ease.

When attending a noble master who possesses compassion and the oral instructions, one is at ease.

When understanding that the sugata essence is present in all the six kinds of beings, it is easy to feel that they are your close relatives.

When you cut through attachment, you are at ease in whatever you do.

When appearance and existence are spontaneously freed, it is easy to discover great bliss.

When knowing sights and sounds to be illusory, it is easy to cut through misery.

When you recognize your natural face, it is easy to be free from effort and struggle.

When thoughts are recognized as dharmata, it is easy to use whatever you see as meditation.

Understanding these, you will be at ease in whatever you do.

Sentient beings of the dark age who never depart from ego-clinging have no happiness. They are all to be pitied.

WAYS OF HAPPINESS

The master said: If you are able to follow these instructions, there are ways to be happy.

The lady asked: What should we do?

The master said: Since there is no bottom to the mud hole of attachment and clinging, you will be happy if you give up your homeland.

Since there is no end to study and reflection upon fields of knowledge, you will be happy if you realize your mind.

Since ordinary empty talk is never exhausted, you will be happy if you can keep silent.

Since the activities of worldly distractions are never brought to an end, you will be happy if you can stay in solitude.

Since there is never an end to activities, you will be happy if you can give up actions.

Since there is never contentment with accumulated wealth, you will be happy if you can cast away attachment.

Since your hated enemies can never be subdued, you will be happy if you can overcome your own disturbing emotions.

Since relatives to whom you are attached can never be satisified, you will be happy if you can cut through your longing.

Since the root of samsara is never cut, you will be happy if you can cut through ego-clinging.

Since thoughts and concepts are never exhausted, you will be happy if you can cut through thought activity.

In general, sentient beings who are not free from ego-clinging have no happiness. They suffer for a long time in the realms of samsara.

GOING ASTRAY

Master Padma said: There are many yogis who stray and become commoners after having taken their pledge.

The lady asked: What does that mean?

The master said: The yogi has gone astray who talks about the view without having recognized the nature of mind and aims at the view in all other directions.

The yogi has gone astray when he imprisons his mind and, without understanding, engages in "stupidity-meditation."

The yogi has gone astray when he claims that everything is mind and then engages in frivolous conduct.

The lady asked: How does one avoid going astray?

The master said: The yogi has not gone astray when he recognizes appearances to be mind and takes dharmakaya as the path.

The yogi has not gone astray when he cuts through all mental constructs and possesses the confidence of the view.

The yogi has not gone astray when he applies this in practice and takes awareness as the path.

The yogi has not gone astray when he understands that appearances are helpers and is free from attachment and clinging.

In any case, in the age of degeneration most yogis go astray. There are few who do not.

SOMETHING UNAVOIDABLE

Master Padma said: When practicing the Dharma, some important things are unavoidable.

The lady asked: What does that mean?

The master said: When you recognize the coemergent wisdom that is present within yourself, there is no way to avoid attaining enlightenment.

When you recognize the characteristic of samsara to be a continuous misery and turn your mind away form it, there is no way to avoid being liberated from samsara.

When you hold no prejudice toward philosophical schools, there is no way you can avoid gaining boundless learning.

When you recognize that the characteristic of samsarsa is continuous suffering and turn away from it, there is no way you can avoid being freed from samsara.

When you have not separated yourself from grasping and fixation, there is no way to avoid falling back into samsara.

Since wisdom does not possess any concrete form, when you know how to clear the five poisons spontaneously, there is no way you can end up in the hells.

There is no one here who possesses these methods, so all will be wandering in samsara for a long time.

LACK OF ATTAINMENT

Master Padma said: The way people are practicing the Dharma will bring no attainment.

The lady asked: What does that mean?

The master said: When giving teachings, they stray into exaggeration and denigration.

When studying, they stray into hope and fear.

When presiding over a feast offering, they stray into clinging to food and drink.

When meditating, they stray into dullness and agitation.

When creating merit, they stray into seeking respect and material gain.

When gaining skills of knowledge, they stray into greater craving.

When linked to many disciples, they stray into being tense about their Dharma practice.

There are too many practitioners who go against the Dharma in whatever they do.

SELF-CONCEIT

Master Padma said: These so-called Dharma practitioners have great ambition in their arrogance and self-conceit.

The lady asked: What does that mean?

The master said: Some have self-conceit regarding themselves as possessing knowledge in learning and teaching.

Some have self-conceit regarding themselves as pious and practicing the Dharma.

Some have self-conceit regarding themselves as meditators who live in the solitude of mountain dwellings.

Some have self-conceit regarding themselves as powerful and as having great abilities.

Some yearn like a carnivorous animal smelling blood when seeing wealth or a desirable object.

When seeing something that is undesirable or harmful, they run away like a wild yak set free.

They are fascinated by their own virtues as when they behold the eye of a peacock feather.

They envy the virtues of others like a watchdog guarding property.

In any case, these conceited Dharma practitioners are their own archenemy. I feel pity for such ignorant people who are in the grasp of Mara.

CUTTING THROUGH THE COMPLEXITY OF GOOD AND EVIL

Master Padma said: When practicing the Dharma, it is necessary to cut through the complexity of virtuous and evil deeds.

The lady asked: What does that mean?

The master said: When conceptual thoughts that hold the notion of an ego are exhausted, there are no Dharma, no evil deeds, no karma, and no ripening of karma. Then you have cut through the complexity of virtuous and evil deeds.

This being so, until you bring an end to the thoughts that hold the notion of an ego, unvirtuous actions will accumulate karma and yield results. Virtuous actions will also accumulate karma and bring results.

When conceptual thoughts are exhausted, there will be no accumulation of good or evil deeds and no results whatsoever will be brought about. This is called "the exhaustion of causes and conditions." It is also called "the ultimate truth."

In the future, during the five hundred years of degeneration, some people will indulge in coarse negative emotions, because of not recognizing ego-clinging and failing to diminish their conceptual thoughts.

Professing to hold the ultimate view, they will claim that being careful about the effects of virtuous and evil actions is a low view.

Belittling the law of karma, they will claim that their minds are enlightened.

There will be some people who act in a frivolous and unrestrained manner.

Their conduct is perverted and will lead both themselves and others in the wrong direction.

Do not follow their example for even one instant!

I, Tsogyal, an ignorant woman, served the nirmanakaya master for a long time. On different occasions, he gave advice on Dharma practice that I persistently retained in my perfect recall, collected, and wrote down for the sake of future generations.

Since they were not meant to be spread at the present time, I concealed these teachings as a precious treasure. May they meet with worthy and destined people.

This "Cycle of Teachings Through Questions and Answers" was committed to writing in the Upper Cave at Chimphu on the twenty-fifth day of the second month of fall in the Year of the Sow.

Seal of treasure.
Seal of concealment.
Seal of entrustment.

ཁཐརྨ་གཏེརྨ་བྱིན་རླབས་ཀྱི༔ དབྱིངས་རྫོགས་ཤ་ས་ག་ཁི་ཏ་ན༔

ཿ ཁྱབ་བདག་ཆེན་པོ་རྡོ་རྗེ་འཆང་ཆེན་ ཿ ཡི་དམ་ལྷ་བསྒྲུབ་པ་ཿ

The Vajra Master and the Yidam Deity

The Teachings to Lady Tsogyal
Oral Instructions on the Secret Mantra

Questions and Answers on the Characteristics
of a Master and How to Meditate on
a Yidam Deity

NAMO GURU.

First, Padmakara, the great master from Uddiyana, was born from a lotus flower. Next he accomplished the vidyadhara level of life.[1] Finally he reached the supreme attainment of mahamudra.[2] He could perceive as many sugatas as there are stars in the sky and was skilled in compassionate means.

Because of his compassion for Tibet, a Dharmaless country shrouded in darkness as if in a dense fog, he went there. He constructed Glorious Samye at Red Rock in order to fulfill the wish of Trisong Deutsen, a bodhisattva on the eighth bhumi.

He practiced sadhana in the Dregu Cave at Chimpu and remained in meditation. During this time he was attended by King Trisong Deutsen, who served him well. Lady Tsogyal of Kharchen also served him and was his personal attendant. Vairocana of Pagor translated all the Dharma teachings from the language of Uddiyana into Tibetan.

Learned and virtuous Tibetans requested teachings from the

---

1. The second of the four vidyadhara levels.
2. The third of the four vidyadhara levels.

master. In particular, Lady Tsogyal, the princess of Kharchen, persistently requested advice on the oral instructions concerning practice and on how to clear away her doubts about the Dharma.

Lady Tsogyal asked the master: Great Master, the master and teacher is of the greatest importance when entering the door of the Secret Mantra teachings. What should be the characteristics of the master whom one follows?

The master replied: The master and teacher is of sole importance. The characteristics of a master are these: He should have trained his mind, he should possess many oral instructions, he should have vast learning and experience in practice and meditation. He should be stable-minded and skilled in the methods of changing the minds of others. He should have great intelligence, and care for others with compassion. He should have great faith and devotion toward the Dharma. If you follow such a master, it is like finding a wish-fulfilling jewel; all your needs and wishes will be fulfilled.

Lady Tsogyal asked the master: Without receiving empowerment from one's master, will one attain accomplishment or not?

The master replied: To exert yourself in study and so forth without attending a master and without having received the empowerments, you will have no result and your efforts will be wasted.

Empowerment is the entrance to the Secret Mantra. To enter the Secret Mantra without the empowerments being conferred is pointless, since it will yield no result and your stream of being will be ruined.

Lady Tsogyal asked the master: If a master himself has not been conferred empowerments and he gives them to others, will they receive the empowerments or not?

The master replied: Although you may be appointed by a charlatan to the rank of a minister thus entrusted with power, you will only meet with misfortune. Likewise, although you may have an empowerment conferred upon you by a master who himself has not received it, your mind will be ruined. Moreover you will destroy the minds of others and go to the lower realms like cattle yoked together falling into an abyss. Carried away within an iron box with no exits, you will be sent to the bottom of hell.

Lady Tsogyal asked the master: Isn't the offering of a gift when receiving empowerment just something you yourself have invented?

The master replied: All the teachings and tantras explain that at this present time when you have obtained the fortune of a human body after being on errant paths for innumerable aeons, you should, free from the three spheres of concepts, offer your body, life, and spouse to the master who shows the path of unexcelled enlightenment.

Lady Tsogyal asked the master: How severe is the misdeed of breaking the master's command?

The master replied: The misdeeds of the three levels of existence do not match even a fraction of the evil of breaking the command of your master. Through this you will take birth in the Unceasing Vajra Hell and find no liberation.

Lady Tsogyal asked the master: How should we regard the master possessing the oral instructions from whom we request teachings?

The master replied in verse:

> You should know that the master is more important
> Than the buddhas of a hundred thousand aeons,
> Because all the buddhas of the aeons
> Appeared through following masters.
> There will never be any buddhas
> Who have not followed a master.

> The master is the Buddha, the master is the Dharma.
> Likewise the master is also the Sangha.
> He is the embodiment of all buddhas.
> He is the nature of Vajradhara.
> He is the root of the Three Jewels.

> Keep the command of your vajra master
> Without breaking even a fraction of his words.

If you break the command of your vajra master,
You will fall into the Unceasing Vajra Hell
From which there will be no chance for liberation.
By serving your master you will receive the blessings.

Lady Tsogyal asked the master: Which is more important, the master or the yidam deity?

The master replied: Do not regard the master and the yidam as different, because it is the master who introduces the yidam deity to you. By always venerating the master at the crown of your head you will be blessed and your obstacles will be cleared away. If you regard the master and yidam as being different in quality or importance you are holding misconceptions.

Lady Tsogyal asked the master: Why is it important to practice the yidam deity?[3]

The master replied: It is essential to practice a yidam deity because through that you will attain siddhis, your obstacles will be removed, you will obtain powers, receive blessings, and give rise to realization. Since all these qualities result from practicing the yidam deity, then without the yidam deity you will just be an ordinary person. By practicing the yidam deity you attain the siddhis, so the yidam deity is essential.

Lady Tsogyal asked the master: When practicing a yidam deity, how should we meditate and practice in order to attain accomplishment?

The master replied: Since means and knowledge are to practice the spontaneously present body, speech, and mind through the method of yoga sadhana, they will be accomplished no matter how you carry out the sadhana aspects endowed with body, speech, and mind. They will be accomplished when the sadhana and recitation are practiced in a sufficient amount.

---

3. The question has been reconstructed since it was missing in the original manuscript.

Lady Tsogyal asked the master: How should we approach the sugata yidam deity?

The master replied: Realize that you and the yidam deity are not two and that there is no yidam deity apart from yourself. You approach the yidam deity when you realize that your nature is the state of nonarising dharmakaya.

Lady Tsogyal asked the master: Which yidam deity is better to practice, a peaceful or a wrathful one?

The master replied: Since means and knowledge are practicing the spontaneously present body, speech, and mind through the method of yoga sadhara, all the countless sugatas, peaceful and wrathful, chief figures and retinues, manifest in accordance with those to be tamed in whichever way is necessary—as peaceful and wrathful, chief figures and retinues. But as they are all of one taste in the state of dharmakaya, each person can practice whichever yidam he feels inclined toward.

Lady Tsogyal asked the master: If we practice one yidam deity, will that be the same as practicing all the sugatas?

The master replied: The body, speech, and mind of all deities are manifested by the three kayas in accordance with the perception of those to be tamed. In fact, no matter how they appear, if you practice one you will be practicing them all. If you accomplish one you will have accomplished them all.

Lady Tsogyal asked the master: Is there any fault in practicing one yidam deity and then practicing another?

The master replied: Although the sugatas manifest as various kinds of families and forms, out of skillful means to tame beings, they are in actuality inseparable, the state of equality. If you were to practice all the buddhas with this realization of their inseparability, your merit would be most eminent. But if you were to do so while regarding the yidam deities as having different qualities which should be either accepted or rejected, you would be immeasurably obscured. It is inappropraite to regard the yidams as good or bad, and to accept

or reject them. If you do not regard them like that, it will be excellent
no matter how many you practice.

Lady Tsogyal asked the master: Through performing the
approach[4] to one tathagata, will we accomplish the mind of all
sugatas?

The master replied: By practicing with a vast view and remaining
in the innate nature, you will attain stability in a yidam deity. When
you complete the recitation, you will accomplish the activities of all
the victorious ones without exception by simply commencing them.

Lady Tsogyal asked the master: If one's view is high, is it
permissible to dispense with the yidam deity?

The master replied: If you attain confidence in the correct view
then that itself is the yidam deity. Do not regard the yidam deity as
a form body. Once you realize the nature of dharmakaya you will
have accomplished the yidam deity.

Lady Tsogyal asked the master: How should my body appear as
the mandala of the deity and how should I train in the two families?

The master replied: To visualize your body as the mahamudra[5] of
the deity's form is to visualize your mind-essence in the form of the
deity.

Since your mind-essence manifests in various ways, as chief figures
and retinues, however they may appear, they are all the magical
display of the enlightened mind of buddhahood.

Lady Tsogyal asked the master: Wrathful deities trample noble
beings such as Brahma, Indra, and the guardians of the world corners
beneath their feet. Will meditating like that not result in transgressions?

The master replied: That is shown as a symbol or indication in

---

4. In general this word (*bsnyen pa*) simply means "recitation" but in particular
the first of the "four aspects of approach and accomplishment."

5. In this context, *mahamudra* means the "sublime bodily form" of a deity.

order to relinquish the clinging to self and others, to trample thoughts into dharmadhatu, and to outshine the arrogance of conceited beings. To regard them as being used as concrete seats is ignorant and confused.

Lady Tsogyal asked the master: Is there any difference in the degree of virtue of meditating on wrathful deities with three heads and six arms and so on, or with just one head and two arms?

The master replied: When wrathful deities have many heads and arms, their three heads symbolize the three kayas, their six arms symbolize the six paramitas. The four legs symbolize the four immeasurables, and their various attributes symbolize the annihilation of vicious beings as well as numerous other qualities. In actuality these forms do not have any substantial nature.

When the deities have one head and two arms, their single head symbolizes the unchanging dharmakaya and their two arms symbolize accomplishing the welfare of beings through means and knowledge. Their two legs symbolize space and wisdom, both manifest and abiding, for the benefit of beings. However you visualize the deities, dharmakaya is beyond any difference in quality and size.

Lady Tsogyal asked the master: What should we do to have a vision of the yidam deity?

The master replied: Do not regard the yidam deity as a form body; it is dharmakaya. The meditation on this form body as manifesting from dharmakaya and appearing with color, attributes, ornaments, attire, and major and minor marks should be practiced as being visible while devoid of a self-nature. It is just like the reflection of the moon in water. When you attain mental stability by practicing like this, you will have a vision of the deity, receive teachings, and so forth. If you cling to that you will go astray and be caught by Mara. Do not become fascinated or overjoyed by such visions since they are only the manifestations of your mind.

Lady Tsogyal asked the master: If we have a vision of one yidam deity, will that be the same as having a vision of all the sugatas?

The master replied: If you have a vision of one yidam deity, it is the same as having a vision of all deities because dharmakaya is beyond quantity.

You will have a vision of whichever deity you are practicing because your mind is becoming pliant. Since the deity is a manifestation of our mind it does not exist anywhere else.

Lady Tsogyal asked the master: When it is said that one attains the level of a vidyadhara through practicing a deity, what does *vidyadhara* mean?

The master replied: Through meditating on your body as being the "sublime bodily form" (mahamudra) by means of self-cognizant intelligence, you will attain the deity of your realized mind-essence endowed with major and minor marks and superknowledges. It is a mahamudra form belonging to whichever family you have practiced. That is called vidyadhara.

Lady Tsogyal asked the master: Where do the vidyadharas dwell?

The master replied: It is your own mind that is dwelling in the form of a deity and it dwells in the manner of nondwelling. Yet is is said that once you reach a vidyadhara level, you will be beyond falling back.

Lady Tsogyal asked the master: How should we venerate the yidam deity?

The master replied: You should venerate the yidam deity by not giving up the yidam deity even at the cost of your life, by not holding doubts about the yidam deity, by not separating yourself from the yidam for even an instant as long as you have not attained the unexcelled mind of enlightenment. By visualizing the deity when you walk, lie down, or sit, you will automatically receive the siddhis and blessings.

Lady Tsogyal asked the master: Is it necessary to practice the yidam deity continuously? Once you accomplish one method is it still necessary to practice?

The master replied: When first practicing a yidam deity and following a sadhana text, even if you have a vision of the yidam deity and receive teachings, it will be a major transgression if you then discontinue the practice. It is therefore essential to practice continuously.

Lady Tsogyal asked the master: How should we continuously practice the approach and accomplishment of the yidam deity?

The master replied: When practicing a yidam deity, you should practice the development stage in each session. Perform the recitation in each session, make offerings, give tormas, make praises, and request the fulfillment of your wishes. Seal the practice in emptiness with the completion stage.

At best do eight sessions a day, as second best do four sessions. At the least, do one session a day. Any less is not permissible. Through that your samayas are fulfilled, and you will receive the siddhis.

When you attain stability in development and completion without discarding your body it will be matured into a deity. That is called the vidyadhara level of maturation. Although your body remains as an [ordinary] human being, your mind is matured into a deity. This is like an image formed in the mold.

When leaving your body in the bardo state, you become that particular deity just like the image coming out of the mold. That is called the vidyadhara level of mahamudra. The body of a practitioner is called an encasement, and the moment the body is discarded, the practitioner becomes the form of the yidam deity.

Lady Tsogyal asked the master: Why are some deities shown as having the heads of animals on bodies of deities? Isn't that meditating on the deity as having substantial existence?

The master replied: The deities manifested with heads of animals symbolize the particular quality which that animal possesses. It is not the case that real and substantially existent deities with animal heads are to be accomplished from somewhere else; they are the manifestations of your own mind.

Emanated from the deities in union are the offspring alloys

(*tramenma*) with animal heads, such as the Eaters and Killers of Kilaya or the eight alloy goddesses (*tramenmas*) of Yangdag. Just as a mixture of gold and silver is called an alloy (*tramen*), these are emanated as having the body of a deity with the head of an animal. They are emanated through the compassion of the male deity and the knowledge of the female deity, or from the male deity who is the nature of means and the female deity who is the nature of knowledge. Symbolizing the particular activity they fulfill, they are manifested as having the head possessing that particular quality.

Lady Tsogyal asked the master: Isn't it conflicting to place supramundane and mundane deities together such as when the chief deity who is supramundane is surrounded by a retinue of mundane deities?

The master replied: The chief figure who is supramundane is a wisdom deity. Like a powerful king he brings conceited beings under his command. The visualized retinues of mundane deities are the deities who carry out his commands and consequently liberate enemies, obstructing forces, and so forth. Supramundane and mundane are like a king and his attendants, so there is no conflict.

Lady Tsogyal asked the master: Is concentration or recitation more important for daily practice?

The master replied: For the accomplishment of the supreme siddhi of mahamudra, when your mind is pliable your concentration will be pliable, and then in actuality you will meet the form of the deity. By recognizing that the deity is your own mind, the three kayas will dawn within yourself.

For the accomplishment of common siddhis, the countless activities of pacifying, increasing, magnetizing, subjugating, and so forth, the mantras are most important. Consequently, complete the set number of recitations. Until you finish retreat it is essential not to interrupt your practice with ordinary talk. No matter what task you may accomplish, you should persevere in the mantras; be very persevering.

Lady Tsogyal asked the master: If one accomplishes the yidam deity that is naturally present, is there any accomplishment?

The master replied: The yidam deity manifests as the unobstructed activity of the compassionate means of all the sugatas. Therefore, in the perception of the sentient beings to be tamed, they appear as peaceful and wrathful, mandalas and buddha-fields, male and female, chief figures with retinues and single figures. The palace of the deity, the chief figure, the retinue, and so forth, in the abode of Akanishtha, are therefore unlike other abodes of gods. The form kayas manifest from the state of nonarising dharmakaya for the benefit of beings and are perceived in accordance with their particular inclinations.

Lady Tsogyal asked the master: In regard to making offerings of tormas and so forth to the deity, if the deity accepts the offerings and is pleased by the praises, it is the same as a substantially existent mundane god. If not, what is the use of performing those deeds?

The master replied: The wisdom deity is not delighted by praises or pleased by offerings. In order to purify your mind, you visualize and invite the deity, make praises, offerings, and so forth. By so doing, your devotion purifies your mind. Due to the unceasing compassionate means of the sugatas you will receive the blessings and siddhis. This is like the following example: by making offerings to a wish-fulfilling jewel, it will fulfill the needs and wishes of sentient beings even though it has no intention to benefit them.

Tsogyal, Tibetan practitioners set aside the deity present in themselves and seek the buddha in Akanishtha. Without even an atom of concentration, their activities stray into shamanistic incantations. Not knowing how to naturally purify their three poisons, they offer tormas of flesh and blood. Without practicing for accomplishment of the supreme siddhi, they desire magical powers, offspring, and wealth. Misapplying the Secret Mantra they divulge its secrets. Bartering the oral instructions like merchandise, they busy themselves with magic and evil spells. Many of them will be reborn as people with wrong views, rudras, yakshas, and rakshas. So perfect the power of the view, practice with concentration, engage in the four activities as your conduct, and accomplish the fruition, the supreme siddhi of mahamudra.

This ends the oral instructions on the Secret Mantra taught by the Master Padmakara to Lady Tsogyal, the princess of Kharchen, in the form of questions and answers.

Seal of treasure.
Seal of concealment.
Seal of entrustment.

ༀ༔ད྄༔ར྄ུ༔ༀ྄ཧེརེཛ྄ར྄ུར྄ར྄ཿ ༈ རྨ྄ག྄ཅ྄ཀ྄ཐ྄ཿ

Vajrayana Mind Training
The Unexcelled Mind Training of Secret Mantra
Instructions on Practicing a Deity
with Attributes

Namo guru dheva dakini hung.

The great master Padmakara had gained accomplishment in development and completion, and had obtained the empowerment of natural awareness display. He had reached the siddhi of abiding in the bodily form of mahamudra. Within the space of manifestation, he played with the whole of appearance and existence. For the benefit of the present king and the princes as well as for the beings of future generations, he gave Lady Tsogyal, the princess of Kharchen, these real instructions, the Unexcelled Mind Training of Secret Mantra.

Lady Tsogyal said: Emaho, great Master! I request from you the oral instructions on the practice of the deity with attributes. Since one does not attain the siddhis without relying on the yidam deity, how should we practice a yidam deity?

The master said: The meditation on the yidam deity with attributes is of two types: the gradual meditation by a person of lesser mental capacity and the meditation on the nondual body by a person of greater capacity.

The Person of Lesser Mental Capacity

The person of lesser mental capacity should train in the precious mind of enlightenment, bodhicitta. To begin with, you the practitioner, no matter where you dwell, should rinse your hands, mouth, face, and so forth with secret nectar or the water of the vase and sit down in the fully or half-crossed leg position on a comfortable seat.

Then you should direct your mind toward sentient beings of the three realms of samsara who are enmeshed in suffering and the causes of suffering. First form the bodhicitta of thinking: In order to take them all out of samsara, I shall practice the form of the yidam diety! Next cultivate the compassion of feeling pity for all sentient beings, the love of wanting them to be free from suffering, the joy of wanting them to meet with happiness, and the impartiality of wanting them not to be apart from happiness.

Following this, utter the three syllables OM AH HUNG and then assume the pride that you are the yidam deity and visualize the particular seed syllable upon a lotus, a sun, and a moon in the yidam's heart center.

Next imagine that through the rays of light issuing forth from the seed syllable, all the buddhas and bodhisattvas abiding in the ten directions as well as all the gurus, yidams, and dakinis are present in the sky before you. Make prostrations and offerings to them, confess misdeeds, rejoice in their merit, take refuge in the Three Jewels, request them to turn the wheel of Dharma, beseech them not to pass into nirvana, arouse the mind set on enlightenment, and dedicate the roots of virtue. Request the masters and the others to depart and let your visualization subside or dissolve into yourself, whichever is suitable. These steps are all aspects of gathering the accumulation of merit.

Following this, in order to gather the accumulation of wisdom, let your entire body become the nature of light by means of rays of light shining from the seed syllable in your heart center. Also radiate light in the ten directions through which all worldly things as well as all beings become the nature of light. This light is then blessed by all the buddhas and bodhisattvas of the ten directions.

As to absorbing the light back into yourself, the world becomes light that is absorbed into the beings, they dissolve into yourself, and the light of your own body dissolves like the vapor of breath on a mirror. That dissolves gradually into the lotus seat, then into the sun and moon, and then dissolves into the seed syllable. The seed syllable then gradually dissolves into the crescent and the bindu. The light of the bindu is of the nature of mind, the size of one part of a hair tip split one hundred ways. Imagine this again and again.

When your visualization is unclear, utter the shunyata mantra and so forth, after which you let the visualization vanish.

The fruition of the two kayas results from perfecting these two types of accumulation.

From within the state of emptiness, imagine that your mind-essence is present as the seed syllable of the yidam deity or imagine that the seed syllable is transformed into a symbolic attribute marked with the seed syllable. From the transformation of this, create the complete head, attributes, and so forth of your particular yidam deity and then the seed syllable upon a sun or moon disc on the lotus in its heart center.

The rays of light shining forth therefrom invite all the sugatas, gurus, yidam deities, and dakinis of the ten directions in the sky before you. Present them then with the five kinds of offerings. Summon the wisdom deities and request them to be seated.

Imagine that the sugatas confer the empowerments upon you and crown you with the lord of the family. Request them then to take leave.

Following this, visualize the three seed syllables upon sun discs in the three centers of your crown, throat, and heart. Consecrate them as being body, speech, and mind. Focus your mind one-pointedly on the yidam deity.

When you then feel weary of meditating, do the recitations.

1. The whispering vajra recitation is to recite so that only your collar can hear it.

2. The melodious vajra recitation is to recite with a tune as at the time of a great accomplishment practice.

3. The secret vajra recitation is to recite mentally.

4. The wheellike recitation is to imagine that it emerges through your mouth, enters the navel, and dissolves back into the heart center.

5. The garlandlike recitation is to spin the mantra garland around

the seed syllable in the heart center and recite one-pointedly while focusing your mind on the syllables.

6. The recitation focused on sound is to recite while focusing your mind only on the sound of the mantra.

PRACTICES DURING BREAKS

Lady Tsogyal asked the master: What should we do in the breaks between meditating on the yidam deity?

The master advised: When you cannot do recitations, then offer tormas and make praises after sounding the bell. Having requested the wisdom deity to take leave, remain as yourself with your ordinary conceptual thinking.

When you, the practitioner, then wish to make offerings for accomplishment, place a painting, statue, or scripture in front of you and make a mandala with scented water strewn with flowers. In one instant, assume the pride of being the yidam deity and send forth rays of light from the seed syllable in your heart center. Invite all the dharmakaya and form kayas dwelling in the ten directions. Request the dharmakaya to remain in the shrine object and scripture. Request the form kayas to remain in the painting and statue.

Imagine that unfathomable assemblies of the buddhas and bodhisattvas, masters, yidams, and dakinis who dwell in the ten directions are remaining before you. Presenting them with any offerings you have, perform the seven purities in front of them.

At this point you can offer tormas to the yidam deity. To the Dharma protectors give water tormas, make tsa-tsa, clay images, or other such practices.

Then if you wish to read the words of all the sugatas, imagine that in an instant your tongue becomes emptiness, from which appears a HUNG and from that a one-pronged vajra. Imagine that the reading issues forth from your seed syllable through the tube of the vajra. Innumerable replicas of your body fill the billionfold universe, each one having a vajra in its mouth. Imagine that the reading is heard by all sentient beings and that they are liberated from samsara. That was the ritual for reciting the sutras.

All these steps are Dharma practices to perform during the breaks or when doing your daily activities.

SEALING THE DEVELOPMENT STAGE

Lady Tsogyal asked the master: How should we seal the development stage with the completion stage?

The master advised: The practitioner who wishes to practice the completion stage shoud, having visualized himself in the form of the deity, request the wisdom deity to take leave. Melting the samaya being into light, it becomes the seed syllable of the deity or a HUNG. The HUNG gradually dissolves and becomes the bindu. The bindu grows smaller and smaller and then becomes clear emptiness. From within this state, remain in the "thatness of all phenomena," empty, nonconceptual self-cognizance beyond the extremes of existence and nonexistence. Alternately, remind yourself again and again in accordance with the oral instructions on the completion stage you have received from your master.

If you, the practitioner, do like that, practicing three or four sessions daily, you will, within this life or without being interrupted by other rebirths, rest in the great yoga during the intermediate state and attain the mahamudra form of the yidam deity. Even if the power of your development stage is not fully perfected, you will in the next rebirth abide in the great yoga state and without a doubt attain the vidyadhara level of mahamudra.

All these steps were advices in progressive stages of meditation for people with simple mental capacities.

THE PERSON OF THE HIGHEST MENTAL CAPACITY

Lady Tsogyal asked the master: How should a person with the highest mental capacity practice?

The master replied: When a person of the highest mental capacity meditates on a deity, he does not visualize it step by step. Simply by uttering the essence mantra, a sentence, or simply by wanting to and thinking of the deity, he visualizes it vividly, instantaneously, and self-existing, like a bubble emerging from water. This is itself the invitation of the deity from dharmadhatu.

To visualize yourself as the deity is space, and that the deity is visible while devoid of self-nature is wisdom. Thus it is indivisible space and wisdom.

The relative is to appear unceasingly as the deity, while the ultimate is to realize that the essence of the deity, devoid of self-nature, is empty. Thus it is the indivisible relative and ultimate.

The deity manifesting as male is means, when manifesting as female it is knowledge. Thus it is indivisible means and knowledge.

The deity manifesting in the form of the deity is bliss, its lack of self-nature is emptiness. Thus it is indivisible bliss and emptiness.

The deity manifesting in the form of the deity is awareness, its appearance devoid of self-nature is emptiness. Thus it is indivisible awareness and emptiness.

The deity manifesting in the form of the deity is luminosity, its lack of self-nature is emptiness. Thus it is indivisible luminosity and emptiness.

Visualizing yourself in that way as the deity, the body aspect is visible yet devoid of self-nature and is therefore beyond age and decline. The speech aspect is unceasing and thus the essence mantra is beyond cessation. The mind aspect transcends birth and death and is thus the continuity of dharmata.

Not being apart from the deity during the four aspects of daily activities—walking, moving about, lying down, or sitting—that is the path of the person of the highest mental capacity. It is extremely difficult and is the domain of someone who possesses the residual karma of former training.

THE STAGES OF VISUALIZING

Lady Tsogyal asked the master: Please give advice on how to keep the deity in mind when meditating on the yidam deity.

The master replied: First, the oral instructions on visualizing the deity: Whether you meditate on the deity in front of you or whether you meditate on yourself as the deity, after having received the master's oral instructions, the master should have given you, the disciple, his blessings and protected you against obstructing forces.

Next, sit on a comfortable seat and be physically at ease. Take a well-made painting of the yidam deity and place it in front of you. Sit for a short time without thinking of anything whatsoever and then look at the image from head to foot. Look again gradually at all the details from the feet to the head. Look at the image as a whole. Sometimes rest without thinking about the image and refresh yourself. Then in this way, look again and again for a whole day.

That evening take a full night's sleep. When you wake up look again as before. In the evening do not meditate on the deity but just rest your mind in the state of nonthought.

Following this, the deity will appear vividly in your mind even without meditating. If it does not, look at its image, close your eyes, and visualize the image in front of yourself. Sit for as long as the visualization naturally remains. When it becomes blurry and unclear, look again at the image and then repeat the visualization, letting it be vividly present. Cut conceptual thinking and sit.

When meditating like this you will have five kinds of experiences: the experience of movement, the experience of attainment, the experience of habituation, the experience of stability and the experience of perfection.

1. When your mind does not remain settled at this time and you have numerous thoughts, ideas, and recollections, that is the experience of movement. Through that you approach taking control of the mind. This experience is like a waterfall cascading over a steep cliff.

2. Then when you can visualize the deity for a short time with both the shape and color of the deity remaining vivid and clear at the same time, that is the experience of attainment. This experience is like a small pond.

3. Following this, when the deity is clear whether you meditate upon it from a long or a short distance, and when it remains for a sixth of your session without any occurrence of gross thoughts, that is the experience of habituation that is like the flow of a river.

4. Next, no thoughts move and you are able to maintain the session

while clearly visualizing the deity. That is the experience of stability that is like Mount Sumeru.

5. Following this, when you can remain for a full day or more without losing the vivid presence of the deity's arms and legs even down to the hairs on its body and without giving rise to conceptual thinking, that is the experience of perfection.

Practitioner, apply this to your own experience!

If you sit too long with an unclear visualization of the deity, your physical constitution will be upset. You will become weary and consequently unable to progress in your concentration. You will have even more thoughts, so first refresh yourself and then continue meditating.

Until you attain a clear visualization, do not meditate at night. In general it is important to visualize in short sessions. Meditate while there is sunlight, when the sky is clear, or with a butter lamp. Do not meditate when you just have woken up or when you feel sluggish or hazy.

At night, get a full night's sleep and meditate the next day in eight short sessions.

When meditating, if you leave the session abruptly you will lose concentration, so do it gently.

When your visualization becomes vivid the moment you meditate, you can also practice at nighttime, during dusk and early dawn.

In general do not weary yourself. Focus your mind on the visualization, grow accustomed to it with stability, and visualize the complete form of the deity.

PROLONGING THE VISUALIZATION

Lady Tsogyal asked the master: For what duration should we remain visualizing the deity?

The master replied: After you have attained some clarity and a slight degree of stability as explained above, the duration of remaining can be prolonged. Usually the recitation determines the length of the sessions. But since the time for recitation has not yet arrived, the duration of your sessions should be according to your ability to remain visualizing.

For the inner measure of sessions, the intervals of breathing are the most important. However, for the outer measure, time and number of sessions is most important.

The measures for sessions can be determined by keeping four sessions each day and night, for as long as possible. The purpose of measured sessions is to not upset your physical constitution, to keep a balanced practice, to enhance your concentration, and to be able to visualize for a long time.

As for counting, do not count verbally but use a mental rosary. Following this, gradually increase the number; take rest for one period and meditate one period.

For the shadow measure, divide the day into sixteen or eight sessions and meditate for every second part of the lines of the shadow. Rest for each part in between. In short, meditate in eight short sessions and alternate by resting in eight.

When you have become stable in this, meditate in two short sessions and gradually prolong them. Then you will be able to remain for a day, a day and a night, half a month, a full month, and so forth.

In short, no matter how stable your session is, the main point is to not weary yourself. So keep proportional sessions, and naturally prolong the duration of unmoving clarity free from thought activity.

These were the oral instructions on prolonging the visualization of the deity.

CORRECTING FAULTS

Lady Tsogyal asked the master: When meditating on the deity how should we correct the faults of transfiguration?

The master said: In order to correct the faults of transfigurations there are two aspects: identifying the faults and correcting the faults.

Regarding identifying the faults, there are two kinds: general and particular.

The general faults are forgetting the visualization, laziness, apprehension, dullness, agitation, too much effort, and lack of effort.

1. Forgetting the visualization is distraction from the meditation.
2. Laziness is indolently thinking, "I will do it later."

3. Apprehension is fearing that you will fail to accomplish and be sidetracked.

4. Dullness is feeling dull because of circumstances, incidentally or naturally.

5. Agitation is feeling naturally agitated, because of either circumstances or a deliberate activity.

6. Too much effort is being discontent while the visualization of the deity is clear and giving rise to further thinking by visualizing it again.

7. Lack of effort is remaining indifferent while the visualization of the deity is unclear.

When meditating on the deity there are the following twelve particular faults: haziness and cloudiness, up and down reversed, the proportions of the body changing, the attire changing, the shape changing, the number changing, the posture changing, the body colors changing, appearing as just color, appearing as just shape, sitting sideways, and gradually vanishing.

Now to explain the methods for correcting these faults. For the seven general faults you should adhere to the eight applications that remove them.

Apply mindfulness when forgetting the visualization. Apply faith, determination, and diligence as the antidote to laziness. Apply right thought as the remedy against apprehension. As the antidote for dullness, develop enthusiasm, take a bath, and walk about. When agitated, develop sadness for samsara, tie your mind with the rope of mindfulness, and bind it to the tree of the visualization. In short, for dullness and agitation use the watchman of alertness. Apply equanimity when you desire to use too much effort. Visualize diligently when you lack effort.

As for correcting the particular faults of the deity, look at the image in detail when hazy, murky, or cloudy, and practice having meditated on nonconceptual emptiness. Alternate among nonthought, looking at the deity, and meditating.

When the proportion of the body or the attire, posture, or shape change, imagine that the body is of material substance and extremely huge and steady. Imagine that pigeons fly in and out of the nostrils, and that birds, sheep, and deer frolic on the arms and legs. Imagine that it remains of solid matter like a statue.

If the number changes, confine the visualization to one or two deities. When it appears as just color, visualize its shape. If it changes color to red or yellow according to the heat of your physical constitutions of blood or bile and so forth, take rest. If it gradually vanishes, focus your mind clearly on the face and arms. For the fault of incompleteness, meditate vividly on the body in its entirety with all the ornaments and attributes.

In short, practice without becoming weary from any of the faults that may arise. Following this, meditate upon nonconceptual emptiness. Then practice while looking at and focusing on the form of the deity.

These were the oral instructions on correcting the faults when meditating on the deity.

TRAINING WITH THE DEITY

Lady Tsogyal asked the master: When training with the deity, how should we train?

The master advised: The oral instruction on training with the deity is to visualize the deity through meditating on nonthought until you are free from these faults. Meditate while alternating the deity and nonthought. When you can visualize the deity without faults, depart from nonthought and meditate exclusively on the deity.

Now for training with the deity. When you can visualize the deity without faults, visualize it as standing upright or sitting or lying on its back or face down, on a plain or a mountain peak, close by or far away, in the center of a rock or at the bottom of water. Train in visualizing the deity in any of these ways whenever you wish to practice.

MINGLING WITH THE DEITY

Lady Tsogyal asked the master: When mingling with the deity, how should we mingle?

The master advised: Once you have trained in the deity and grown accustomed to it, dissolve it into yourself. Visualize it whether you are a single deity or a mandala with a buddha-field. Then in order to connect the deity to the ultimate, the deity is visualized by your own thoughts and then stabilized. Your mind and the eight collections of consciousness are what manifest as bodily form and the wisdom of the deity. Ultimately, it is the awareness of enlightened mind, the great self-existing wisdom, the essence of fruition. The deity does not appear from elsewhere. No matter how it appears, it is devoid of a self-nature and is therefore a nondual form. To appear in the form of the deity is beyond attachment since its vajra-like body, speech, and mind are manifest while devoid of self-nature.

Although your mind manifests as the deity, it has no self-nature. Since it cannot be examined or demonstrated as being such and such, it is dharmakaya.

You the practitioner, who have thus trained in this meaning, should observe and abide by the six samayas of the practice. You should not break off your devotion for the master who has given you the oral instructions. Apply what is conducive to samadhi and avoid what is not conducive. Do not let your concentration dissipate during daily activities. Carry on to perfection without abandoning the yidam, keep the particular deity you practice secret and do not meditate with the frame of mind that rejects one deity in order to accept another. Any deity you practice is the same as meditating on all the buddhas. The buddhas are nothing to be meditated upon besides realizing your own mind. Even the visualization of the yidam deity is a mental manifestation. Apart from that there is nothing to accomplish or meditate upon. The buddhas and bodhisattvas are embodied within your yidam deity. Although you may meditate on many yidam deities, they are still manifestations of your mind. If you meditate on just one, that also is a manifestation of your mind.

These were the oral instructions on mingling with the deity and connecting it to the ultimate.

HOW TO ACCOMPLISH THE DEITY

Lady Tsogyal asked the nirmanakaya master: How does one take a deity as the path and accomplish it?

The master replied: To accomplish a deity, first visualize the deity being in front of you. Then stabilize the visualization of yourself as the deity. Up to this point, avoid doing the recitations.

Now, when about to practice the deity, arrange a mandala for accomplishment and set out offerings. Place the shrine objects in front of you and, having refreshed yourself, sit down on a comfortable seat.

Invite your master and the assembly of yidam deities, make prostrations, offerings, and praises, and perform the eight branches. The deities then melt into light and dissolve into yourself, by which method you visualize yourself as the yidam deity. Draw the boundary lines for retreat and sanctify the offerings.

By means of the three samadhis and so forth, visualize the mandala together with the deities. Perform the consecration and empowerment. Invite and absorb the wisdom deity and make homage, offerings, and praises.

Again, visualize the wisdom deity in front of you, separate from yourself, and do the recitation. When you have finished reciting, make praises.

Absorb the deity separate from yourself back into yourself and go to sleep while retaining the pride that you are the deity.

Visualize the deity instantly the next morning and make recitations following your sadhana text as above.

Sanctify your food and drink and offer it as a feast.

In this way whether you train with the yidam deity to be an assembly of mandala deities or a single form, you will still accomplish it.

This was the oral instruction for accomplishing the deity.

THE SIGNS OF ACCOMPLISHMENT

Lady Tsogyal asked the master: When accomplishing a deity, what signs and indications of accomplishment will appear?

The master advised: There are four kinds of signs: marks, dream omens, indications, and actual signs.

The four types of marks are like smoke, mirage, fireflies, and a cloudless sky. These are explained as being examples for progressive stages of experience.

The five types of dream omens are as follows: seeing buddhas and bodhisattvas as different from oneself, seeing the buddhas and oneself as equal, seeing oneself in the form of the deity without front and back, seeing that all the buddhas and bodhisattvas pay homage and make offerings to oneself, and dreaming that all the buddhas impart and explain profound teachings.

Moreover, to dream repeatedly that one is naked is a sign of having purified habitual tendencies. To dream of ascending a staircase into the sky is a sign of having entered the path. To dream of riding on lions and elephants is a sign of having achieved the bhumis. Dreaming of a smiling apparition and so forth is a sign of receiving a prophecy.

Even if you do have such excellent dreams, do not be exhilarated.

There are outer, inner, and secret indications of practice.

1. The outer indications during meditation are: to see material objects such as subtle particles, seed syllables, mind attributes, subtle bodily forms, and so forth, or to see gross perception spheres of five colors such as of fire and water and so forth.

2. The inner indications are that when meditating on the deity you do not notice the outward and inward movement of your breath, that your body is buoyant like cotton wool, and that you are free from old age and decay.

3. The secret indications are that when you practice the deity as a mere illusory apparition, wisdom is naturally present. You feel equal compassion for everyone and your field of experience dawns as wisdom.

Actual signs are the outer and the inner signs. The outer signs are that lights appear, the image of the deity smiles, a great sound or a sweet fragrance appears, a butter lamp lights by itself, your skull cup levitates, or that you are without any physical discomfort. The inner signs are that your compassion grows greater than before, your attachment diminishes, you are free from prejudice, you have pure samaya and love for your master and Dharma friends, you have no fear of samsara and are not intimidated by Mara.

When many such signs occur, do not become exhilarated but be diligent.

These are the way in which the indications and signs of practicing the deity appear.

THE RESULTS OF PRACTICE

Lady Tsogyal asked the master: Which qualities will result from practicing a deity?

The master said: The qualities resulting from deity practice are that you purify your obscurations and gather the accumulations.

Since your conceptualization is brought to an end by meditating on a deity, you will purify the obscurations of karma, disturbing emotions, and places of rebirth.

As for the gathering of the accumulations, there are five types of results: the path results, which are the four vidyadhara levels, and the ultimate result.

The vidyadhara levels have two aspects: qualities and essence. The qualities are the six superknowledges and the four magical powers. The essence is the four vidyadhara levels, which are the vidyadhara level of maturation, the vidyadhara level of life mastery, the vidyadhara level of mahamudra, and the vidyadhara level of spontaneous presence.

The ultimate result is that when your meditation of the deity becomes pliable, even if you have few qualities and little intelligence, you will without a doubt attain the state of perfect buddhahood.

THE FIVE PATHS

Lady Tsogyal asked the master: It is taught in the system of prajnaparamita that one must proceed through the paths. How should we combine the five paths with practicing the mandala of the deity to perfection?

The master replied: The path of practicing the mandala of the deity as four aspects: the path of joining, the path of seeing, the path of cultivation, and the path of consummation.

These gradual paths can be connected to the four aspects of

approach and accomplishment in that approach is the path of joining, full approach is the path of seeing, accomplishment is the path of cultivation, and great accomplishment is the path of consummation.

THE PATH OF JOINING

The path of joining has four aspects. Practicing the suchness and the magical samadhis is heat. Practicing the subtle concentration and the single form is summit. Practicing the full manifestation and the elaborate form is acceptance. Practicing the assembly on the uninterrupted path is supreme mundane attribute.

1. Through the samadhi of suchness decide that all phenomena are your own mind and practice nonthought in the unfabricated nature of mind. Practice until you realize it.

The magical samadhi is the self-display of nonarising space. That is to practice the cognizant and yet nonconceptual inseparability of manifestation and emptiness. It is like space permeated by light, being cognizant while manifesting and nonconceptual while being cognizant.

When you have realized this after attaining pliancy, you will cross the boundary between the affinities of the greater and lesser vehicles, after which the eleven signs of attaining the heat will appear:

- Insects do not live on your body.
- Your outer and inner defilements are purified.
- You are free from the illnesses of the four compositions.
- You attain physical patience.
- You overcome your own conceptual thinking.
- Free from material food, your radiance and majestic brilliance are beyond waning.
- You do not give rise to ordinary desire.
- You are free from the five disturbing emotions.
- Your habitual tendencies of feeling inclined toward the view and conduct of the lesser vehicles are exhausted.
- You are free from the eight worldly concerns.
- You attain the acceptance of the profound Dharma.

These were the eleven signs of being beyond falling back.

2. To practice the single form and the subtle concentration at the

summit stage is to meditate on the subtle samadhi and the single form until it becomes manifest in the three fields of objects.

The signs of the concentration of the summit are that your five inner disturbing emotions do not arise toward outer objects and that you cannot be harmed by the five outer elements. Those are the signs that your mind has mingled with appearance.

3. Practicing the yoga of the elaborate form at the acceptance stage is to train yourself in the peaceful and wrathful deities as three families, five families, or a given number of groups of families.

You have reached perfection in this when, having grown accustomed to it, you can send forth light with an instantaneous samadhi and your natural awareness can visualize a mandala of even one thousand buddhas.

The signs that you have attained the stage of acceptance and have become pliant in disclosing appearances are that you can transform sand into gold, make water appear in a dry place, make a sprout grow forth from charcoal, and can control all perceivable things as you wish. These are the signs of having attained mastery over mind.

4. Accomplishing the assembly on the uninterrupted path at the stage of supreme mundane attribute is to practice the meaning of the great bliss of dharmata. When you have become extremely stable, you are endowed with the five articles and so forth, and you commence the sadhana at an auspicious time.

If your power of concentration in this is strong, you attain the vidyadhara level of life mastery and thus you will, within six, twelve, or sixteen months, reach the attainment of the sacred family of mastery. Your life force will equal the sun and the moon and you can extend your life span one hundred years at a time.

If your power of concentration is weak, you attain the vidyadhara level of maturation. Having left your body behind, you attain the complete form of the yidam deity in the bardo. That is the result of stability in the development stage.

THE PATH OF SEEING

Now I will explain the full approach as the path of seeing. After you have realized that your residual body is a mental body, your defilements are exhausted and you attain the changeless vidyadhara level of life mastery beyond birth and death, without even leaving your physical body behind. Having attained the five superknowledges and four magical powers, you realize the characteristics of the ultimate. Although you transform yourself into myriad things through three incalculable aeons, display your magical powers on the path of seeing and act for the welfare of beings, you engage in actions without attachment and receive teachings from the nirmanakaya in person. You will be beyond falling back from the paths.

THE PATHS OF CULTIVATION AND CONSUMMATION

Now to explain the accomplishment as the path of cultivation. The path of cultivation is to put the characteristics of the ultimate into practice, having reached the mahamudra level of the rainbowlike body.

Although your state of mind during the meditation state is not different from that of the buddhas, you still retain the state of consciousness of the postmeditation and must therefore deliberately rest in meditation. Because you now abide in unshakable concentration, it is the vidyadhara level of mahamudra. This is the experience of being unshakable from ati yoga. Without moving from the meditation state you send forth myriads of magical apparitions and accomplish the welfare of beings. Mentally or by means of symbols you can receive teachings from the sambhogakaya.

As for the path of consummation of the great accomplishment, the vidyadhara of spontaneous presence, your qualities are almost equal to the supreme qualities of the buddhas, but there is still the difference between whether or not the meditation state brings forth enhancement. The vidyadhara level of spontaneous presence possesses instantaneous enhancement.

Gathering regents and giving teachings, you attain the consummation, the vajra-like samadhi, and accomplish the welfare of self and others through effortless magical powers. This is the action of the expression of wisdom. Meeting the dharmakaya face to face, you receive teachings through blessings and purify the subtle obscuration of dualistic knowledge.

These are the gradual path of how to attain the four aspects of approach and accomplishment, the five paths, and the four vidya-dhara levels.

SKIPPING THE GRADES

Lady Tsogyal asked the master: When explaining the short path of Secret Mantra, is it possible to journey the path by skipping the grades?

The master replied: It is also taught that there is a path that skips grades. It is possible that some people reach consummation, progressing through the paths of joining, seeing, and cultivation simultaneously. Without having to journey step by step, some people attain enlightenment from the path of seeing, some reach buddhahood from the path of cultivation, some journey progressively to the end and then reach the state of buddhahood. People are divided due to their degree of power of intelligence and concentration.

These four ways of practicing the path according to the levels of the four types of people do not depend on following a path after taking rebirth in a future life. The resultant system of Secret Mantra holds that you are freed from the illness of samsara within this very lifetime, and having attained the level of samadhi beyond rebirth, you spontaneously accomplish the three kayas.

In order to reach the bhumi of Indivisibility and attain dharmakaya within a single lifetime, intelligent people are taught to train in the path of dharmakaya, grow accustomed to it, and take thatness as the path.

In order to reach the bhumi of Unexcelled Wisdom and attain the kaya of great bliss, passionate people are taught to train in the path of great bliss, grow accustomed to it, and take bliss as the path.

In order to reach the bhumi of the Great Assembly Circle and attain the form kayas, angry people are taught to train in the path of deliverance and grow accustomed to it. People who hold attributes are taught to take the deity as path.

In this way you purify the realms of the three kayas and grow accustomed to the three bhumis. Since all these results are contained within your own mind, decide that buddhahood does not exist elsewhere.

These are the supreme qualities of the path that skips the grades.

THE KAYAS AND WISDOMS

Lady Tsogyal asked the master: How do we attain the fruition of Secret Mantra, the five kayas, and the five wisdoms?

The master advised: In connection with the different types of capacity just mentioned above, when you have proceeded in the manner of the four ways of taking as path, you attain the ultimate fruition, the spontaneously present result of the five kayas and five wisdoms.

The dharmadhatu wisdom is the fact that this general form of all buddhas, your innate nature devoid of constructs, a primordially unconditioned essence, is the unproduced, unborn, and original purity beyond arising and ceasing.

The mirrorlike wisdom is the fact that although dharmadhatu is devoid of concrete substance, it is by nature luminous and all phenomena appear like reflections in a mirror while having no self-nature, and are cognized while having no conceptual thinking.

The wisdom of equality is the fact that, unceasingly, dharmadhatu is self-existing awareness, and this awareness wisdom is devoid of constructs. Perception is unborn, nondual, and great equality.

Individually discriminating wisdom is the fact that without leaving this nondual state of equality, the general and individual characteristics of phenomena are unmixed and utterly complete, while the habitual tendencies of ignorance are relinquished and omniscient wisdom arises without possessing the misery of conceptual thinking.

The wisdom of the persevering action[1] is to rest while remaining cognizant, as just mentioned. This inseparable wisdom is to accomplish and to perfect the welfare of self and others spontaneously and with perseverance.

---

1. *Bya ba nan tan gyi ye shes.* Usually it is "all-accomplishing wisdom" (*bya grub ye shes*).

These five wisdoms manifest separately as the unceasing expression of your awareness, but they are never apart from the basic wisdom of dharmadhatu. The basis of all, this dharmadhatu wisdom is primordially present in yourself; throughout the three times the practitioner is never apart from it.

Now follows how the five kayas are present.

Dharmakaya is the unfabricated innate nature, a profound naturalness, beyond arising and ceasing, and devoid of constructs.

Sambhogakaya is the enjoyment of the self-existing wisdom of awareness, because the kayas and wisdoms are present within the continuity of the innate nature of your mind.

Nirmanakaya is compassion born out of wisdom, magically displayed and manifest in all ways.

The great bliss kaya is the unborn bliss of enlightened mind.

The essence kaya is the fact that these four kayas are inseparable as the essence of the innate enlightened mind.

Since the five kayas and five wisdoms are spontaneously present, this is called possessing the general form of all buddhas. The practitioner meditates gradually on the essence of these five kayas at the time of the path as being the nature of his own mind. When the practitioner parts with the enclosure of the physical body, he attains these five kayas and five wisdoms in a way that transcends attainment, and perceives them in a way that transcends perception.

Here is the explanation of how buddhahood acts for the welfare of sentient beings. Numerous reflections of the sun appear on the surface of many waters without leaving behind the single circle of the sun. Similarly, the truly and completely Enlightened One, the dharmakaya, without leaving behind the equality of the innate nature, magically appears, through the sambhogakaya and nirmanakaya, in accordance with the particular inclinations of those to be tamed in a number as great as the infinite space. Although acting for the benefit of beings, the dharmakaya holds no conceptual thinking.

For example, the sunlight does not conceive of benefiting beings. In the same way the two kayas hold no concepts of acting for the welfare of beings. The welfare of beings results from the power of aspiration.

The master advised: Tsogyal, when the five hundred-year cycle of the dark age arrives, most followers of Mantra will only utter the words rather than practice their meaning. They will let the Secret Mantra stray into shamanistic incantations and will misuse the samaya substances for hollow rituals. They will build their hermitages in the center of the village. Claiming to be practicing union, they will indulge in ordinary desire. Claiming to be practicing deliverance, they will indulge in ordinary anger. Confusing good with evil, they will barter the oral instructions and even the teachers will sell them to the disciples. They will turn the Secret Mantra into speculation and will practice with political incentive and self-centered ambition.

In this final period, the Secret Mantra will be obscured by words. The blessings of the Secret Mantra will diminish because of lack of understanding its meaning. Since only few attain siddhi, there will come a time when the Secret Mantra is close to vanishing. For the sake of a destined person endowed with the residual karma at that time, write down this hearing lineage and conceal it as a treasure.

In the High Soaring Cave at Yerpa, on the twenty-second day of the last autumn month in the Year of the Monkey, I, Lady Tsogyal, wrote down this jewel garland of oral instructions, the Mind Training of Secret Mantra, and concealed it as a treasure. After meeting with a destined person endowed with the residual karma, may these words purify the obscurations for his wisdom and may he attain the vidyadhara level.

Treasure seal.
Concealment seal.
Profundity seal.
Entrustment seal.

ཤྱགར་ལྕུགས་ཕྲེང་།

The Crystal Garland of Faultless Practice

NAMO GURU.

When the great master Padmakara, a mantradhara who possessed a blessed tradition of teachings, was staying at the hermitage Pearl Crystal of Pamagong, Lady Tsogyal, the princess of Kharchen, requested instructions. On that occasion, he taught this Crystal Garland of Faultless Practice for the benefit of future generations. People in future times, pay heed to this!

The nirmanakaya master Padma said: When practicing the Dharma from your heart, you need to have a qualified master who is authentic and trustworthy, a perfect spiritual teacher with the unbroken transmission of a pure lineage.

If your teacher is fake, the instructions will be mistaken and all your training will become perverted. Since that would be extremely dangerous, it is essential to meet with a qualified master. Keep that in mind!

Lady Tsogyal asked: What is meant by unbroken transmission of the lineage?

The nirmanakaya master replied: One needs a lineage that is the unbroken transmission of enlightenment from dharmakaya, sambhogakaya, and nirmanakaya. The lineage of Master Padma is like that. Dharmakaya Samantabhadra transmitted to sambhogakaya Amitabha, who transmitted awareness through skillful means to nirmanakaya Padmakara. You, woman, have received the words of the nirmanakaya in person. You are endowed with the transmission of the lineage as well as its blessings.

The nirmanakaya master Padma said: The teachers should not give the heart advice to unsuitable disciples who lack the karmic link.

Lady Tsogyal asked: What is meant by that?

The master replied: Such people do not respect their teacher and cunningly try to obtain the teachings. Having received them, they designate the teachings to a different source and let the oral instructions go to waste. They do not uphold the command of the lineage. Since they do not practice, to give them the profound teachings is the same as throwing pure gold dust in the gutter. Such disciples are not a suitable vessel for the instructions. Since they do not comprehend and will lack conviction, they will be unable to retain the teachings. By giving the oral instructions to unsuitable people, the teachings will become nothing but written words and books, thus distorting the Dharma. By giving them to an improper recipient, the teachings will be spoiled. There is no need for that. It is essential to be able to maintain the profound teachings and to skillfully examine the character of the disciples. Keep that in mind!

The nirmanakaya master said: Do not teach the Dharma to people who create misconceptions.

Lady Tsogyal asked: What defect does this have?

The master replied: Such unsuitable people have no understanding of the vital points of oral instruction. Since they lack the transmission of the lineage, their mind will not mingle with the Dharma and their character will become corrupt. Teaching the Dharma to people who are skilled in dry intellectual speculations and cling to mere words of sophistry will result in slandering the Dharma. By slandering the Dharma the slanderer will accumulate evil karma, and you yourself, by being angry, will also gather misdeeds. Thus both teacher and recipient will gather evil karma through the Dharma. There is no need for that.

Do not make the profound instructions into a sales item but practice with perseverance in remote places and mingle your mind with the Dharma.

The nirmanakaya master Padma said: Do not keep followers who let the instructions go to waste.

Lady Tsogyal asked: What does that mean?

The master replied: Businessmen who take delight in worldly gain and reputation are occupied with their daily needs, and do not let practice become their main pursuit. They are satisfied with just having "practiced," "received," or "understood" the Dharma. At the prospect of obtaining a mere trifle of gain or fame, food or wealth, enjoyment or respect, they will not retain the teachings, even though they have the guru's command of secrecy. Instead they will carelessly expound the teachings mixed with falsehood and charlatanism. Do not impart the oral instructions to followers or disciples who, like charlatans, will use their teacher and the Dharma. The Dharma teachings will become spoiled. There is no need to give the nectar of immortality to others without having drunk yourself, and only give it to people with sincere interest. By corrupting the profound teachings of Secret Mantra one will not receive any blessings, the mother and sister dakinis will be annoyed, and obstacles will result. Keep that in mind!

The nirmanakaya master said: Extract the nectar of the oral instructions and give it to worthy people who possess the karmic continuity of former practice, who wish to pursue the sacred meaning from the core of their heart, and who will practice it with perseverance.

Lady Tsogyal asked: What does that mean?

The master replied: Such people, regarding their master as a buddha, have great devotion. Perceiving the oral instructions to be nectar they feel conviction. Since their mind is free from doubt and hesitation they regard the teachings as a precious, wish-fulfilling jewel. Perceiving the misery of samsaric activities as poison they exert themselves in practice for the sake of the future. Seeing the pursuits of this life as futile they have great fortitude and perseverance when trying to accomplish the unexcelled enlightenment. Such noble people who are untainted by the faults of competitive and ambitious craving for material gain and prestige are the sublime spiritual offspring of the victorious ones. If you impart the instructions in full to such people, it will be of benefit to both yourself and others. Keep that in mind!

An improper vessel cannot hold the milk of a snow lion. Yet when poured into a jar of gold, it has wondrous properties.

The nirmanakaya master said: If you wish to attain enlightenment within one lifetime but do not enter the path of self-discipline, the practice will not be taken to heart. It is therefore essential to engage in self-discipline.[1]

Lady Tsogyal asked: How does one enter the path of self-discipline?

The master replied: When first practicing the Dharma, if you do not practice with self-discipline but are indolent, lazy, and pretentious, you will have no success. For this reason, go to a retreat place such as a charnel ground, a highland area, a snow mountain, a remote hermitage, the dwelling place of a siddha, or a forest in auspicious months such as the seasons of summer and autumn, or on auspicious days such as the eighth day or the new and full moon days.

At such a place you should sweep, make a seat, prepare a mandala, lay out offerings, and arrange the shrine with representations of enlightened body, speech, and mind. Present a torma to the local deity of the place, the nagas and others, and with a drink offering, command them to refrain from making obstacles and to be virtuous companions.

The next morning give up idling. Engage instead in Dharma activities such as making offerings to the master and the Precious Ones, making supplications and presenting tormas to the yidam, dakinis, and Dharma protectors. When presenting the tormas, do not cast them facing in an outward direction, but facing toward yourself, as an auspicious coincidence for not letting the siddhis slip away.

In the daytime you should train in regarding your perceptions as

---

1. Literally "willing to bear hardship," *self-discipline* here does not have the negative connotation of penance or self-mortification; it means keeping to a simple life-style in solitude while undertaking the "hardship" of avoiding worldly pursuits and comfort.

being dreams. That is to say, rest naturally and relaxed without correcting what appears. Leave your experience spontaneously free and open. Rest wide awake and without fixation.

During evening time you should take awareness as the path. That is to say, heighten awareness at the close of day and rest alertly and wakefully without falling subject to drowsiness and stupor.

At midnight mingle the state of deep sleep with dharmata and sleep in the state of nonthought. Apply the strong determination of thinking, I will recognize my dreams to be dreams! Through that you will be able to remember dharmata while dreaming and be liberated from elation or nightmare.

At morning time you should take dharmata as path. That is to say, when you awake from sleep and your body feels at ease, bring dharmata to mind and practice this self-existing mindfulness without fixating, meditating, or slipping away into drowsiness. Do not give in to indulging in sloth and indolence, but practice wide awake while keeping the right measure of self-discipline.

Until you have completed the retreat, do not wear the clothes of others as that can cause defilement and dissipation of your practice. If your food is too rich you will fall under the power of disturbing emotions. If it is too unwholesome your physical strength will weaken, leaving you incapable of continuing your practice with self-discipline. Keep a measured and balanced diet.

Do not eat unclean, stolen, or thrown away food. Do not eat the food of people with the defilement of violated samaya or of people who are afflicted by evil forces. If you do, accomplishment will be delayed and the obstacle of not completing your retreat may occur.

Do not move your seat. If you do move your seat or bed before the completion of your retreat or before the duration of your vow has expired, the signs and indications will disappear and you may meet with sudden obstacles.

Do not perform rituals for the protection of others or try to do exorcism; if you do your capabilities will decrease. Do not wash the dirt off your body, clothes, head, and hair, since that will cause the siddhis to fade and vanish. Do not cut your hair, beard, or nails since that will weaken the power of mantra. Do not expound the Dharma to others from inside your retreat hut as that will impede the signs of accomplishment. Do not take your vow or pledge to practice for an extended period just once, but take it daily, otherwise you may be influenced by Mara.

The power of mantra does not develop through having conversations with others, so keep silence of speech. If you chant the vajra recitations of Secret Mantra or wrathful deities with a loud voice, their powers will diminish and nonhumans and spirits will panic and faint. So chant them correctly in a whispering tone of voice.

If you recite while lying down, counting the mantras with your hand on your chest, you will only encumber yourself. In all cases, when you sit with straight body the channels will be straight, which will let the winds circulate freely. Since the winds and the mind are interconnected, when the winds flow freely the effect is that your mind will be able to remain focused and concentrated. Therefore, it is for a most profound reason that you should keep the body in the seven points of meditation posture.

Do not sleep during the daytime. This will bring numerous defects so give it up by all means.

Do not spit or throw mucus in places frequented by people since that will impede the power of mantra.

Until you have completed retreat practice give up actions of benefiting others, pursuits, and distractions, or deeds that are disturbing for your body, speech, or mind; concentrate with perseverance on your practice while increasing virtuous actions for your own benefit.

While continuing retreat, no matter what good or evil signs of practice or magical displays may occur, do not become involved in like or dislike or in judging what to accept and what to reject. Practitioner, let your mind rest in its natural state and continue the practice to the end.

When finishing retreat, perform the offerings of thanksgiving, loosen the restrictions of your retreat, but retain the retreat condition for a few days without going to the town or far away. For three days, do not sleep in any other place than your own bed and stay out of the sight of people who do not share the same samaya.

Do not show your practice material to others and do not share the substance of accomplishment,[2] but partake of it yourself.

From the start of retreat practice until completion, do not suddenly rush out of retreat, no matter what happens. Identify it as the obstacle of Mara and do not give in to difficulties.

In all cases, a practitioner exerting himself in approach and accomplishment should not haphazardly engage in daily activities. Do not eat any food you come by. Do not put on grimy or defiled garments. Do not lie down just anywhere to sleep. Do not defecate in the sight of others or where people walk. Do not engage in untimely acts of yogic discipline. At all times be most careful in your behavior.

In general, if you desire happiness, carry through with your Dharma practice, undertaking self-discipline and accepting unpleasant conditions. Divide your days and nights into parts and practice in measured sessions. Your happiness will then be long lasting. Keep that in mind!

The nirmanakaya master said: When trying to attain unexcelled enlightenment, if you cannot keep your vow for an extended period of time you will be influenced by the demon of obstacles.

Lady Tsogyal asked: What does that mean?

The master replied: When you have vowed to practice the uncorrupted oral instructions, ardently apply the remedies to rid yourself of attachment to the flattery of others and to the fetters of food and drink that result from others' respect, bowing, making offerings to you, and asking for protection ceremonies. That only interrupts the spiritual practice of someone who is lacking in stability and confidence.

Initially you can take the vow for three, seven, or nine days, or for half a winter month or one summer month, and then gradually extend it to months and years. Best is to pledge to practice for twelve years, next best for six years, and the least is three years or one year. If, unable to accomplish even that, you can keep to this discipline,

---

2. The offering articles of the feast performed on the morning of the last day of retreat practice.

employing your body, speech, and mind to nothing but spiritual pursuits, and practice for as much as six months, a summer or winter season, without laziness and indolence, it will be most meaningful and you will enter the path of enlightenment.

In general, vows that one cannot keep are the greatest cause for transgression. Therefore do not take any vows that you will be unable to keep. Make only promises or vows that are in accordance with your own ability. To practice in that way is more profound. Keep that in mind!

The nirmanakaya master said: At the time of assimilating your master's authentic oral instructions through practice, it is important always to keep silence of speech, the retreat of your voice.

Lady Tsogyal asked: What does that mean?

The master replied: Of all the distractions, the greatest is useless chatter. Consequently, unconnected empty talk is fatal to spiritual practice. Being able to keep silent is the most excellent retreat; it keeps you undisturbed even when remaining in a marketplace.

Regardless of how much self-discipline you practice, to keep silence is decidedly best. If you are unable to do that, you should at least keep silence until the completion of your practice period. Through keeping silent and not interrupting your spiritual practice with ordinary talk, you will achieve powers of speech and swiftly attain accomplishment.

In general, much talk that is not Dharma practice or concerning Dharma is meaningless. There is no need for that. If you do not strive toward unexcelled enlightenment with your voice engaged in reciting and chanting after stopping ordinary talk, you are anyway like a mute. Keep that in mind!

The nirmanakaya master Padma said: When meditating on the yidam deity, it is essential to realize the composure of body, speech, and mind.

Lady Tsogyal asked: What is meant by that?

The master replied: To visualize your body as the form of the deity, apparent yet without concrete existence, is the composure of body. To let your speech resound the mantra of the deity, distinctly and clearly as resounding emptiness, is the composure of speech. Your mind, pure and free from conceptual thoughts, the unity of cognizance and emptiness, is the composure of mind. Not to be apart from the composure of body, speech, and mind is called mahamudra.

When you continuously recite these three syllables that are the essence of the sugatas; OM for body, AH for speech, and HUNG for mind, you are endowed with the body, speech, and mind of all the sugatas.

In general, if you remain without separating yourself from enlightened body, speech, and mind, your practice of Secret Mantra is definitely safe from taking an errant path. Keep that in mind!

Master Padma said: It is essential to keep the measure of time for sessions with the number of recitations.

Lady Tsogyal asked: What does that mean?

The master replied: When doing recitations, designate each of the three or four parts of the day a session, and vow to recite both day and night, at best one thousand, at the second best five hundred, or at least one hundred and eight recitations.

Until completing that number, keep silence and do not interrupt your recitation with ordinary talk. In this way no obstacles will arise.

To combine the stages of development and completion and to exert yourself in approach and accomplishment like the steady flow of a river is the special quality of authentic practice of the oral instructions.

All that you can aspire toward such as purifying the obscurations, gathering the accumulations, clearing away obstacles, and swiftly attaining the twofold siddhis will be easily accomplished through combining the stages of development and completion with the recitation of approach and accomplishment.

Of all types of recitation, recite the three syllables, OM AH HUNG, which are the essence of body, speech, and mind of all the sugatas. They are the most profound and all-inclusive. Therefore it brings great blessings to pledge to recite them or to append them at the head of all other mantra recitations.

In general, gathered drops can become an ocean. Do not allow your lips to be idle but continuously gather even single syllables of mantra. This is most important. Then at some point there will be accomplishment. Keep that in mind!

Master Padma said: Without uniting means and knowledge, Secret Mantra will stray onto an errant path.

Lady Tsogyal asked: What does that mean?

The master replied: *Means* refers to the unmistaken principle of what one is practicing, whether it be at the stage of development or completion. *Knowledge* refers to the view, the meaning of empty dharmata, and self-existing luminosity. Without realizing that the view is the self-existing empty cognizance within yourself, you are not entering the path of knowledge. Through knowledge devoid of means you will not have any experience, and through means devoid of knowledge, dharmata is not put into practice. It is therefore necessary to unite them without letting them be separated.

In general, to separate means and knowledge is like a bird trying to fly with only one wing; you cannot reach the level of buddhahood. Keep that in mind!

Master Padma said: Without practicing the nonduality of meditation and postmeditation, you will not achieve the abode of emptiness.

Lady Tsogyal asked: What does that mean?

The master replied: During meditation you rest in the inconcrete essence of dharmata, cognizant but without conceptual thinking. During postmeditation, you realize everything to be empty, without self-nature. Free from attachment to or fascination for the experience of emptiness, you will naturally progress beyond meditation and postmeditation and be free from holding a conceptual focus or conceiving of attributes, just as clouds and mist spontaneously clear in the vast expanse of the sky.

In general, during both meditation and postmeditation, your meditation on the nature of dharmata should be beyond clarity and obscuration, like observing a figure in a mirror.

Master Padma said: If you cannot practice by naturally clearing away drowsiness and agitation, you will fall into the extremes of their faults, despite your meditation.

Lady Tsogyal asked: What does that mean?

The master replied: At the time of meditation, resting in the natural state of dharmata, by looking into drowsiness, agitation, and so forth at the moment they occur, you will see that drowsiness itself is empty dharmata. When agitated look into the agitation itself and you will see that the object of agitation is also empty.

When the attachment to casting away drowsiness and agitation has been cleared and you no longer cling to them as being concrete, drowsiness and agitation will be spontaneously freed without falling into their extremes. When you can practice this natural clearing away of drowsiness and agitation, then self-existing meditation has taken place.

In general, since all meditations are involved in trying to correct drowsiness and agitation, they become conceptual meditations. It is essential to realize that the root of drowsiness and agitation is emptiness. Keep that in mind!

Master Padma said: If you cannot mingle the Dharma with daily life activities, you will be fettered by the meditation session.

Lady Tsogyal asked: How does that fetter one?

The master replied: The dharmata devoid of constructs that you experience in your being while resting evenly in meditation should be put into practice in every situation during postmeditation; whether walking, moving around, lying down, or sitting. By never separating from this Dharma practice no matter what daily activity you perform, you will always remain in the state of dharmata. Thus your meditation will transcend sessions.

In general, the meditator who imprisons his body and mind without applying the vital points of meditation is fettered by a chain. Keep that in mind!

Master Padma said: You will not purify the obscurations of karma by setting aside the practices of offering and confession.

Lady Tsogyal asked: What does that mean?

The master replied: At the time of putting the oral instructions into practice, you should do what is called "taking Dharma activities as one's path." That is, you should transform into an unconditioned path the Dharma activities of meditation, making offerings, circumambulation, making tsa-tsa and tormas, reading aloud, chanting, copying texts, and so forth. Perform these activities incessantly. Through clinging, tiredness, and so forth, you do not accomplish the main objective.

In general, if you do not embrace the practice with nonconceptualization, whatever virtuous acts you perform will merely produce the effect of samsaric happiness: they will not become the path of enlightenment. That would be pointless.

Therefore, it is essential to perform any elaborate virtuous actions of body, speech, and mind while in a state free from conceptions. Keep that in mind!

Master Padma said: If you do not perfect the signs through practicing the Dharma, the instructions have not truly taken effect.

Lady Tsogyal asked: What is meant by that?

The master replied: The inner signs are that bliss, clarity, and nonthought dawn from within you. Free from clinging to concreteness and fixating on disturbing emotions, your thoughts are self-liberated.

The middle signs of discovering the blessings of the Dharma are when blessings spontaneously manifest within your body and speech, when you are able to cut through negative emotions and overcome difficulties, and when sickness, negative forces, and the Maras cannot deceive you.

The outer signs of having freed your mind through Dharma practice are when, free from the eight worldly concerns, the knot of your ego-clinging is untied and falls apart.

In general, certainty will not arise if the Dharma master is incompetent. Therefore it is of utmost importance to connect yourself to a master with an unbroken lineage of wondrous siddhas. Keep that in mind!

Master Padma said: Profound instructions have no books.

Lady Tsogyal asked: What does that mean?

The master replied: When an extraordinary master imparts a profound instruction, even through one single sentence, to a worthy disciple who puts it into practice, the disciple will give rise to certainty and will accomplish the result.

Tsogyal, your unborn mind is empty, luminous, and all-pervasive. Experience it constantly.

In general, if the Dharma master is excellent you will have profound instructions wherever you go. Keep this in mind!

Master Padma said: No matter which teaching you practice, if it is not for the benefit of sentient beings then that practice will lead to the shravaka's state of cessation.

Lady Tsogyal asked: How will it lead to that?

The master replied: When putting the oral instructions into practice, you practice the buddha-mind in order to attain enlightenment for the benefit of all sentient beings. It is to accomplish the benefit of others. That is not the aim of the general vehicles. To wish for one's own peace and happiness, emancipation and liberation, belongs to the lesser vehicle.

In general, wishing peace for oneself alone is the cause of suffering. That is pointless.

People whose practice is only self-seeking will rarely find happiness. It is therefore essential to exert yourself only for the welfare of others. When practicing for the sake of others you may be free from self-interest but your own benefit will be spontaneously accomplished. Keep that in mind!

Master Padma said: If you do not embrace your practice with nonconceptual compassion, all the roots of virtue that you have performed will go to waste.

Lady Tsogyal asked: How is that?

The master replied: A root of virtue that is conceptual cannot be multiplied and thus will be exhausted. If a virtuous action is embraced by nonconceptual dedication, that root of virtue is inexhaustible and is therefore the chief cause of unexcelled enlightenment.

What is meant by *nonconceptual*? It means to not conceive of "I," to not conceive of "other," and to not conceive of the root of virtue. Dissolve your conceptions completely into emptiness.

In general, a virtuous root is unerring when embraced by nonconception. To think with a conceptual focus, I did a virtuous action!, and to dedicate your virtuous deeds toward material gain or good reputation, is perverted dedication.

When a good deed done for gain and reputation is combined with a dedication to a similar end, it cannot be multiplied. So in all cases the most important key point is total purity of the three concepts. Keep that in mind!

Master Padma said: One root of virtue with skillful means can outshine all others.

Lady Tsogyal asked: What does that mean?

The master replied: If you want to apply the oral instructions skillfully, then train in the true meaning and give it the seal of nonconceptual dedication. Thereby you will outshine practices of material focus and thus the root of virtue will increase no matter which practice you are performing.

In short, the most important key point is to let your roots of virtue become inexhaustible and to continually increase them until you have attained unexcelled enlightenment. In all cases, completely let go of all focus on dedication, object of dedicating, and dedicator, while leaving no trace behind. Keep that in mind!

The nirmanakaya master Padmakara said: By keeping company with three harmonious companions, you will be immune to the obstacles of Mara.

Lady Tsogyal asked: What does that mean?

The master replied: Generate devotion toward the harmonious authentic master and visualize him always above your head in order to make supplications and offerings.

Keep company with harmonious friends who practice the teachings with the same samaya as yourself, who do not strive for aims or material things of this life, but who are determined to pursue virtuous actions for the sake of the future.

Adhere to the harmonious instructions that are unperverted, and put them into practice through the profound teachings on the stages of development and completion in accordance with the actual application of an accomplished master.

If you remain inseparable from these three, you cannot be harmed by obstacles of Mara.

In general, if you take your own mind as witness that you exert yourself in deeds that will not be despised by the Three Jewels, the lasting result will always be excellent. Keep that in mind!

Master Padma said: When practicing the Dharma it is necessary to lay a good foundation.

Lady Tsogyal asked: How is that to be done?

The master replied: First of all, if you lack the accumulation of merit, you will not meet with the master who possesses the oral instructions. If you lack the karmic continuity of former training, you will not understand the teachings. If you lack the special faith and devotion, you will fail to perceive the virtues of the master. If you lack vows, discipline, and samayas, you will violate the root of Dharma practice. If you are not guided by the oral instructions, you will not know how to meditate. If you lack diligence and perseverance, you will not enter the pathway of practice and your virtue will stray into laziness. If your mind does not sincerely turn away from samsaric pursuits, you will not reach perfection in Dharma practice.

If all these factors coincide, there will be success in Dharma practice. The accomplishment of unexcelled enlightenment depends on the coincidence of many causes and conditions, so be diligent!

In short, in order to abandon what should be abandoned and accomplish what should be accomplished do not leave your body, speech, and mind in ordinariness but exert yourself and the result will be excellent. Keep that in mind!

Master Padma said: It is of no benefit to know about the Dharma. You must take it to heart and put it into practice.

Lady Tsogyal asked: What should one do when practicing?

The master replied: Opening wide the understanding of the view, be without partiality concerning the teachings. Seizing the throne of meditation, condense within your mind the meaning of all the teachings. Opening the entrance gate of action, let there be no conflict between your view and behavior. Possessing the confidence of fruition, let samsara and nirvana be equal as dharmata. Understanding the limits for keeping the samayas, observe the threefold vows. Practicing in this way, your Dharma practice will be free from error.

In general there is no need to let Dharma practice become mere platitude, to not assimilate it in one's heart, and to not apply it in practice. Keep that in mind!

Master Padma said: In the future, when the dark age of degeneration arrives, some people who claim to be practitioners will desire to teach others without having received permission. Without having practiced themselves they will instruct others in meditation. Without being liberated themselves they will pretend to give instructions for liberation. Without being devoid of self-interest they will instruct others to cast away their fetters of attachment and be generous. Without the slightest understanding of the good or evil of their own actions they will spout clairvoyant statements about the good or evil fare of others. Having no stability themselves they will claim to be benefiting other beings. I think there will be many who will pretend, be hypocritical, cheat, and deceive in the name of the Dharma.

All people of future generations who wish to practice the Dharma, read this written testament of the mendicant Padmakara and examine yourself!

Observe the shortcomings of samsaric misery! Since it is evident that all the material things of this life are impermanent, turn your mind toward yourself and think well! Listen to the life stories of how the accomplished masters of the past practiced self-discipline. Find a qualified master and serve him with devoted body, speech, and mind.

At first do not befriend him like an equal acquaintance but cut your misconceptions through learning and contemplation.

Next, keep to constant practice and exert yourself with perseverance.

Finally, assimilate the Dharma in your heart through practice and apply the remedies to disturbing emotions.

Always keep your samayas and disciplines without transgressions. Do not practice intermittently or postpone your practice, but keep your pledge to apply it immediately.

Although I, a mendicant, have attained accomplishment, I have never found time for distraction. On seeing all the lost sentient beings who are tormented by samsaric pursuits and delusions, disturbing emotions and evil karma, I feel like weeping. My heart aches with despair and anguish.

Having obtained a human body and perceived the pleasant or painful results of good or evil actions, people who do not try to attain enlightenment in this lifetime and who do not practice even one session of taking refuge, but instead chase the pursuits, ambitions, distractions, and enjoyments of this life and accumulate evil karmic deeds have no heart. Their hearts have rotted. The demon of Mara has crept into their hearts. They are deceived by demonic friends.

If you entrust yourself to the Three Jewels from the core of your heart and practice to attain enlightenment in one lifetime, it is impossible that you will be deceived by the Three Jewels.

It is also impossible that you will suffer from want of food and clothing. The people who claim to lack food or clothes for Dharma practice, who have no time for taking refuge or spiritual practice and say that they have found no leisure, are shamelessly fooling themselves.

Right now, while your senses are clear and you have free time, if you do not exert yourself in the practices for attaining enlightenment you will very soon be blown away by the wind of karma, approached by the demonic Lord of Death, and be in danger of imminent death. At that time you will frantically try to think of all possible things but it will be far too late. Keep that in mind!

In general, when practicing the Dharma you will have no success unless you keep death in mind.

Capable people of future generations, there is no deception in these words of the mendicant Padmakara. No matter what you pursue, try hard to be free from regret at the time of death! Take care of yourselves and be diligent with the aspiration to also be able to help others!

This teaching entitled The Grystal Garland of Faultless Practice, the heart essence manifest as the nectar of immortality, was requested from the nirmanakaya master Padmakara, with respectful and devoted body, speech, and mind, by me, Kharchen Tsogyal.

For the sake of future generations, I composed it in writing and concealed it as a treasure since it was not to be propagated.

Having met with the fortunate one, may it be put into practice.

This was the teaching on the Immaculate Crystal Garland of Faultless Practice.

> Seal of treasure.
> Seal of concealment.
> Seal of entrustment.

The Refined Essence of
Oral Instructions

Lady Tsogyal of Kharchen served the nirmanakaya Orgyen Padmakara from her eighth year, accompanying him as a shadow follows
a body.

When the master was about to leave Tibet for the land of the
rakshas, I, Lady Kharchen, having offered a mandala of gold and
turquoise and having turned a wheel of gathering,[1] implored: Oh,
Great Master! You are leaving to tame the rakshas. I am left behind
here in Tibet. Although I have served you for a long time, master,
this old woman has no confidence about the time of death. So I
beseech you to kindly give me an instruction condensing all teachings
into one, which is concise and easy to practice.

The great master replied: Devoted one with a faithful and virtuous
mind, listen to me.

Although there are many profound key points of body, rest free
and relaxed as you feel comfortable. Everything is included in simply
that.

Although there are many key points of speech such as breath
control and mantra recitation, stop speaking and rest like a mute.
Everything is included in simply that.

Although there are many key points of mind such as concentrating,
relaxing, projecting, dissolving, and focusing inward, everything is
included in simply letting it rest in its natural state, free and easy,
without fabrication.

---

1. A feast offering *(ganachakra),* which has the value of certain measures of gold.

The mind doesn't remain quietly in that state. If one wonders, Is it nothing?, like haze in the heat of the sun, it still shimmers and flashes forth. But if one wonders, Is it something? it has no color or shape to identify it but is utterly empty and completely awake—that is the nature of your mind.

Having recognized it as such, to become certain about it, that is the view. To remain undistracted in the state of stillness, without fabrication or fixation, that is the meditation. In that state, to be free from clinging or attachment, accepting or rejecting, hope or fear, toward any of the experiences of the six senses, that is the action.

Whatever doubt or hesitation occurs, supplicate your master. Don't remain in places of ordinary people; practice in seclusion. Give up your clinging to whatever you are most attached to as well as to whomever you have the strongest bond with in this life, and practice. Like that, although your body remains in human form, your mind is equal to the buddhas'.

At the time of dying, you should practice as follows.

By earth dissolving in water, the body becomes heavy and cannot support itself. By water dissolving in fire, the mouth and nose dry up. By fire dissolving in wind, body heat disappears. By wind dissolving in consciousness, one cannot but exhale with a rattle and inhale with a gasp.

At that time, the feelings of being pressed down by a huge mountain, being trapped within darkness, or being dropped into the expanse of space occur. All these experiences are accompanied by thunderous and ringing sounds. The whole sky will be vividly bright like an unfurled brocade.

Moreover, the natural forms of your mind, the peaceful, wrathful, semiwrathful deities, and the ones with various heads fill the sky, within a dome of rainbow lights. Brandishing weapons, they will utter "Beat! beat!" "Kill! kill!" "Hung! Hung!" "Phat! phat!" and other fierce sounds. In addition, there will be light like a hundred thousand suns shining at once.

At this time, your innate deity will remind you of awareness, saying, Don't be distracted! Don't be distracted! Your innate demon will disturb all your experiences, make them collapse, and utter sharp and fierce sounds and confuse you.

At this point, know this: The feeling of being pressed down is not that of being pressed by a mountain. It is your own elements dissolving. Don't be afraid of that! The feeling of being trapped within darkness is not a darkness. It is your five sense faculties dissolving. The feeling of being dropped into the expanse of space is not being dropped. It is your mind without support because your body and mind have separated and your breathing has stopped.

All experiences of rainbow lights are the natural manifestations of your mind. All the peaceful and wrathful forms are the natural forms of your mind. All sounds are your own sounds. All lights are your own lights. Have no doubt about that. If you do feel doubt, you will be thrown into samsara. Having resolved this to be self-display, if you rest wide awake in luminous emptiness, then simply in that you will attain the three kayas and become enlightened. Even if you are cast into samsara, you won't go there.

The innate deity is your present taking hold of your mind with undistracted mindfulness. From this moment, it is very important to be without any hope and fear, clinging and fixation, toward the objects of your six sense faculties as well as toward fascination, happiness, and sorrow. From now on, if you attain stability, you will be able to assume your natural state in the bardo and become enlightened. Therefore, the most vital point is to sustain your practice undistractedly from this very moment.

The innate demon is your present tendency for ignorance, your doubt and hesitation. At that time, whatever fearful phenomena appear such as sounds, colors, and lights, don't be fascinated, don't doubt, and don't be afraid. If you fall into doubt for even a moment, you will wander in samsara, so gain complete stability.

At this point, the womb entrances appear as celestial palaces. Don't be attracted to them. Be certain of that! Be free from hope and fear! I swear there is no doubt that you will then become enlightened without taking further rebirths.

At that time, it is not that one is helped by a buddha. Your own awareness is primordially enlightened. It is not that one is harmed by the hells. Fixation being naturally purified, fear of samsara and hope for nirvana are cut from the root.

Becoming enlightened can be compared to water cleared of sediments, gold cleansed of impurities, or the sky cleared of clouds.

Having attained spacelike dharmakaya for the benefit of oneself, you will accomplish the benefit of sentient beings as far as space pervades. Having attained sambhogakaya and nirmanakaya for the welfare of others, you will benefit sentient beings as far as your mind pervades phenomena.

If this instruction is given three times to even a great sinner such as one who has killed his own father and mother, he will not fall into samsara even if thrown there. There is no doubt about becoming enlightened.

Even if you have many other profound teachings, without an instruction like this, you remain far away. Since you don't know where you may wander next, practice this with perseverance.

You should give this oral instruction to recipients who have great faith, strong diligence, and are intelligent, who always remember their teacher, who have confidence in the oral instructions, who exert themselves in the practice, who are stable-minded and able to give up concerns for this world. Give them this with the master's seal of entrustment, the yidam's seal of secrecy, and the dakini's seal of entrustment.

Although I, Padmakara, have followed many masters for three thousand six hundred years,[2] have requested instructions, received teachings, studied and taught, meditated and practiced, I have not found any teaching more profound than this.

I am going to tame the rakshas. You should practice like this. Mother, you will become enlightened in the celestial realm. Therefore persevere in this instruction.

Having spoken, Guru Rinpoche mounted the rays of the sun and departed for the land of the rakshas. Following that, Lady Tsogyal

---

2. The years here are the ancient way of counting summer and winter seasons as each one year.

attained liberation. She committed this teaching to writing and concealed it as a profound treasure. She made this aspiration: In the future, may it be given to Guru Dorje Lingpa. May it then benefit many beings.

This completes the Sacred Refined Essence Instruction, the reply to questions on self-liberation at the moment of death and in the bardo.

SAMAYA. SEAL, SEAL, SEAL.

Glossary

This glossary is mainly a compilation of information received as oral teachings from Tulku Urgyen Rinpoche, Chökyi Nyima Rinpoche, and other Buddhist masters of the present times. Some of the entries are short and contain no definition, but since the Tibetan equivalents are included, the reader can seek further clarification from other sources. Some of the English terms were coined exclusively for use in this book and may have been phrased differently in another context.

ACCEPTANCE (bzod pa) One of the four aspects of ascertainment attained on the path of joining.

ACCEPTANCE OF THE PROFOUND DHARMA (zab mo'i chos la bzod pa) Acceptance of emptiness; that dharmas are unproduced.

ACCOMPLISHMENT (1) (dngos grub, siddhi) See Siddhi. (2) (sgrub pa). See Four aspects of approach and accomplishment.

ACCUMULATION OF MERIT (bsod nams kyi tshogs) Virtuous actions with concepts.

ACCUMULATION OF WISDOM (ye shes kyi tshogs) Virtuous actions embraced by the discriminating knowledge (shes rab) of insight into emptiness.

ACCUMULATIONS (tshogs) The provisions for journeying along the path of enlightenment. See Two accumulations.

AGITATION (rgod pa) The state of mind disturbed by thoughts and emotions.

AKANISHTHA ('og min) The highest; the realm of Vajradhara, the dharmakaya buddha. For a discussion of the various types of Akanishtha, see Gyurme Dorje's forthcoming translation of Longchen Rabjam's *Phyogs bCu Mun Sel,* entitled *Dispelling the Darkness of the Ten Directions.*

ALL-GROUND (kun gzhi; Skt. alaya) Literally it means the foundation of all things. The basis of mind and both pure and impure phenomena. This word has different meanings in different contexts and should be understood accordingly. Sometimes it is synonymous with buddha nature or dharmakaya, sometimes it refers to a neutral state of dualistic mind that has not been embraced by innate wakefulness.

AMITABHA (snang ba mtha' yas)   The chief buddha of the lotus family. The manifestation of discriminating wisdom.

APPEARANCE AND EXISTENCE (snang srid)   Whatever can be experienced (the five elements) and has a possibility of existence (the five aggregates). This term usually refers to the world and sentient beings.

APPROACH (bsnyen pa)   *See* Four aspects of approach and accomplishment.

APPROACH AND ACCOMPLISHMENT (bsnyen sgrub)   Two aspects of sadhana practice. Especially phases in the recitation stage according to Mahayoga Tantra.

ARHANT (dgra bcom pa)   "Foe destroyer"; someone who has conquered the four Maras and attained the fourth and final result of the Hinayana path.

ATI YOGA (shin tu rnal 'byor)   The third of the three inner tantras. Same as *Dzogchen.*

BARDO (bar do; Skt. antarabhava)   Intermediate state. Usually refers to the period between death and the next rebirth. For details of the four bardos, see *The Mirror of Mindfulness* (Boston: Shambhala Publications, 1989).

BHUMI (sa)   The levels or stages of the bodhisattvas; the ten stages of the last three of the five bodhisattva paths. *See* Ten bhumis.

BILLIONFOLD UNIVERSE (stong gsum 'jig rten gyi khams)   The domain of a supreme nirmanakaya consisting of one billion Mount Sumerus each surrounded by four continents and rings of mountains.

BINDU (thig le)   In the context of deity yoga, a tiny sphere of light, often the size of a pea.

BLISS, CLARITY, AND NONTHOUGHT (bde gsal mi rtog pa)   Three temporary meditation experiences. Fixation on them plants the seeds for rebirth in the three realms. Without fixation, they are the adornments of the three kayas.

BODHICITTA (byang sems, byang chub kyi sems)   (1) The aspiration to attain enlightenment for the sake of all beings. (2) In the context of Dzogchen, the innate wakefulness of awakened mind.

BODHICITTA OF APPLICATION ('jug pa'i byang chub kyi sems) It is comprised chiefly of the six paramitas.

BODHICITTA OF ASPIRATION (smon pa'i byang chub kyi sems) It is comprised chiefly of the four immeasurables.

BODHICITTA OF UNDIVIDED EMPTINESS AND COMPASSION (stong nyid snying rje dbyer med byang chub kyi sems) Same as "ultimate bodhicitta."

BODHISATTVA (byang chub sems dpa') Someone who has developed bodhicitta, the aspiration to attain enlightenment in order to benefit all sentient beings. A practitioner of the Mahayana path; especially one who has attained the first bhumi.

BODILY FORM OF MAHAMUDRA (phyag rgya chen po'i sku) The "body of mahamudra" refers to the rainbowlike form of one's personal yidam. *See* the chapter on the four vidyadhara levels, "The Vajra Master and the Yidam Deity."

BRAHMA (tshangs pa) The ruler of the gods of the realm of form.

BRAHMA-LIKE VOICE (tshangs pa'i dbyangs) The voice endowed with the perfect qualities of Brahma, the king of the gods.

BUDDHA (sangs rgyas) Enlightened or Awakened One, who has completely abandoned all obscurations and perfected every good quality. A perfected bodhisattva, after attaining true and complete enlightenment, is known as a buddha. The buddha generally referred to is Shakyamuni Buddha, the buddha of this era, who lived in India around the sixth century B.C.E. There have been innumerable buddhas in past aeons who have manifested the way to enlightenment. In the current Good Aeon, there will be one thousand buddhas, of which Buddha Shakyamuni is the fourth.

BUDDHA, DHARMA, AND SANGHA (sangs rgyas chos dge 'dun) The Three Jewels. The true objects of refuge. For more details, *see* Thrangu Rinpoche's book *Buddha Nature* (Rangjung Yeshe Publications, 1988).

BUDDHA NATURE (bde gshegs snying po) Sugatagarbha, the essence of the sugatas; the potential for enlightenment or enlightened nature that is inherently present in each sentient being. For a detailed discussion, see Thrangu Rinpoche's *Buddha Nature*.

BUDDHAHOOD (sangs rgyas) The perfect and complete enlightenment of dwelling in neither samsara nor nirvana.

BUDDHAHOOD OF OMNISCIENCE (rnam mkhyen sangs rgyas kyi sgo'phang) The state of complete enlightenment endowed with the perfect wisdom of seeing the nature of things as they are and with the wisdom of perceiving all that exists.

CHIMPHU (chims phu) The hermitage of caves above Samye in central Tibet. Guru Rinpoche spent several years there in retreat.

COEMERGENT WISDOM (lhan cig skyes pa'i ye shes) The innate wakefulness potentially present in all sentient beings. *Wisdom* here means the primordially undeluded wakefulness.

COMPLETION STAGE (rdzogs rim) *Completion stage with marks* means yogic practices such as tummo. *Completion stage without marks* is the practice of Dzogchen. *See also* Development and completion.

CONCEPTUAL MIND (blo) In this context, the act of our intellect that discerns and classifies phenomena is a hindrance for the naked state of awakened mind that can operate unimpededly without concepts.

CONSECRATION AND EMPOWERMENT (byin brlab dbang bskur) A phase in the development stage at the end of having created the visualization of the yidam deity that involves consecrating one's three higher chakras with enlightened body, speech, and mind as well as empowering the deity with the crown of the five buddha families.

DAKINI (mkha' 'gro ma) One of the three roots. Spiritual beings who fulfill the enlightened activities, female tantric deities who protect and serve the Buddhist doctrine and practitioners.

DARK AGE OF DEGENERATION (snyigs ma'i dus) The present age, when the five degenerations are rampant—those of life span, the era, beings, views, and disturbing emotions. *See also* Five degenerations.

DEITY WITH ATTRIBUTES (mtshan bcas kyi lha) The ultimate deity is the dharmakaya of our own mind. In order to realize this natural state, we use the support of an enlightened being with face, arms, legs, ornaments, et cetera.

DEVELOPMENT AND COMPLETION (bskyed rdzogs) The means and knowledge of Vajrayana practice. The development stage is fabricated by mind. *Completion stage* means resting in the unfabricated nature of mind. *See* Development stage, Completion stage.

DEVELOPMENT STAGE (bskyed rim; Skt, utpattikrama) One of the two aspects of Vajrayana practice that is to create pure images mentally in order to purify habitual tendencies. The essence of the development stage is "pure perception" or "sacred outlook," which means to perceive sights, sounds, and thoughts as deity, mantra, and wisdom. *See also* Development and completion.

DHARMA (chos) The Buddha's teachings; sometimes *dharma* can mean phenomena or mental objects, as well as attributes or qualities.

DHARMA PROTECTORS (chos skyong)   The guardians of the Buddhist teachings.

DHARMADHATU (chos kyi dbyings)   The realm of phenomena; the suchness in which emptiness and dependent origination are inseparable. The nature of mind and phenomena that lies beyond arising, dwelling, and ceasing.

DHARMAKAYA (chos sku)   Of the three kayas, it is the mental or unmanifest aspect. Can be understood differently according to the context of ground, path, or fruition. In this book, it mainly refers to the empty, cognizant, and uncompounded aspect of one's mind at the time of the path. *See also* Three kayas of fruition.

DHARMAPALA (chos skyong)   Nonhumans who vow to protect and guard the teachings of the Buddha and its followers. Dharmapalas can be either "mundane," i.e., virtuous samsaric beings, or "wisdom Dharma protectors," who are emanations of buddhas or bodhisattvas.

DHARMATA (chos nyid)   The innate nature of phenomena and mind.

DHYANA REALMS OF THE GODS (lha'i bsam gtan gyi ris)   A meditative state of concentrated mind with fixation leads not to liberation but to being reborn as a god in the realm of form produced through such mental concentration.

DISCIPLINES (tshul khrims)   *See* Vows and precepts.

DISTURBING EMOTION (nyon mongs pa).   The five poisons of desire, anger, delusion, pride, and envy, which tire, disturb, and torment one's mind.

DUALISTIC FIXATION (gnyis 'dzin)   Experience structured as "perceiver" and "object perceived."

DZOGCHEN (rdzogs pa chen po, rdzogs chen; Skt, mahasandhi, maha ati, Great Perfection)   The teachings beyond the vehicles of causation, the highest of the inner tantras of the Nyingma School, first taught in the human world by the great vidyadhara Garab Dorje. Dzogchen is the ultimate of all the eighty-four thousand profound and extensive sections of the Dharma. It is the realization of Buddha Samantabhadra, exactly as it is. The aspects of means and knowledge of Dzogchen are known as *trekcho* and *thogal*.

EGO-CLINGING (bdag 'dzin)   The habitual clinging to the mistaken idea that the "I" is an independent, singular, and permanent entity. Ego-clinging is the source of disturbing emotions and the basis for all negative karmic actions leading to endless samsaric existence.

EGOLESSNESS (bdag med)   The absence or lack of a self-entity in the individual person as well as in matter and mind. Egolessness is not an achievement but the natural state of things. Practitioners of the lower vehicles, the shravakas and pratyekabuddhas, attain a partial realization of egolessness, but it is the bodhisattva who through practicing the six paramitas discovers reality as it is.

EIGHT BRANCHES (yan lag brgyad)   The seven branches in addition to arousing bodhicitta. *See also* Seven branches.

EIGHT CHARNEL GROUNDS (dur khrod brgyad)   (1) Cool Grove, Sitavana (bsil ba tshal), in the east; (2) Perfected in Body (sku la rdzogs) to the south; (3) Lotus Mound (pad ma brtsegs) to the west; (4) Lanka Mound (lan ka brtsegs) to the north; (5) Spontaneously Accomplished Mound (lhun grub brtsegs) to the southeast; (6) Display of Great Secret (gsang chen rol pa) to the southwest; (7) Pervasive Great Joy (he chen brdal ba) to the northwest; (8) World Mound ('jig rten brtsegs) to the northeast. There are also numerous other lists of charnel grounds.

EIGHT CLASSES OF GODS AND DEMONS (lha srin sde brgyad)   There are various descriptions but the most general is: devas, nagas, yakshas, gandharvas, asuras, garudas, kinnaras, and mahoragas. All of them were able to receive and practice the teachings of the Buddha. These eight classes can also refer to various types of mundane spirits who can cause either help or harm.

EIGHT COLLECTIONS OF CONSCIOUSNESS (rnam shes tshogs brgyad)   The all-ground consciousness, mind-consciousness, defiled mind-consciousness, and the five sense-consciousnesses.

EIGHT WORLDLY CONCERNS ('jig rten chos brgyad)   Attachment to gain, pleasure, praise, and fame, and aversion to loss, pain, blame, and bad reputation.

EIGHTEEN CONSTITUENTS (khams bco brgyad)   The six collections of consciousness, the six senses, and the six sense objects.

EIGHTY-FOUR THOUSAND DOORS TO THE DHARMA (chos kyi sgo mo brgyad khri bzhi stong)   Twenty-one thousand teachings each on vinaya, sutra, Abhidharma, and their combination, sometimes referred to as Vajrayana. Their purpose is to eliminate the eighty-four thousand different types of disturbing emotions latent in one's mind.

EMPOWERMENT (dbang)   The conferring of power or authorization to practice the Vajrayana teachings, the indispensable entrance door to tantric practice.

EMPOWERMENT OF AWARENESS-DISPLAY (rig pa'i rtsal gyi dbang)   The empowerment for practicing Dzogchen. Sometimes it also refers to the realization achieved through Dzogchen practice.

EMPTINESS (stong pa nyid) The fact that phenomena and the ego are empty of, or lack, independent true existence.

ENLIGHTENED ONES (sangs rgyas) Same as *buddhas*.

ENLIGHTENMENT (byang chub; Skt. bodhi) Usually the same as the state of buddhahood characterized by perfection of the accumulations of merit and wisdom, and by the removal of the two obscurations, but sometimes also the lower stages of enlightenment of an arhant or a pratyekabuddha.

ESSENCE KAYA (ngo bo nyid kyi sku; Skt. svabhavikakaya) The "essence body." Sometimes counted as the fourth kaya, the unity of the three kayas. Jamgon Kongtrul defines it as the aspect of dharmakaya that is "the nature of all phenomena, emptiness devoid of all constructs and endowed with the characteristic of natural purity."

ESSENCE MANTRA (snying po'i sngags) The short form of the mantra of a yidam deity as opposed to the longer dharani mantra; for example, *om mani padme hung*.

ETERNALISM (rtag lta) The belief that there is a permanent and causeless creator of everything; in particular, that one's identity or consciousness has a concrete essence that is independent, everlasting, and singular.

EXAGGERATION AND DENIGRATION (sgro btags + skur 'debs) Attaching existence or attributes to something that does not have them, and underestimating the existence or attributes of something that does have them.

EXPERIENCE AND REALIZATION (nyams rtogs) An expression used for insight and progress on the path. *Experience* refers to temporary meditation experiences and *realization* to unchanging understanding of the nature of things.

EXTRACTING ESSENCES (bcud len, Skt. rasayana) A yogic practice of living off the essences of medicinal plants, minerals, and elemental energy in order to purify the body, heighten concentration, and avoid the diversions of seeking ordinary material food.

FIVE AGGREGATES (phung po lnga) The five aspects that comprise the physical and mental constituents of a sentient being: physical forms, sensations, conceptions, formations, and consciousnesses.

FIVE DEEDS WITH IMMEDIATE RESULT (mtshams med pa lnga) The five immediate karmas, sins, or evil acts are killing one's mother, one's father, or an arhant, causing schism in the sangha of bhikshus, and drawing blood from a tathagata with evil intent. The five misdeeds close to or approaching them (de dang nye ba lnga) are defiling one's mother who is an arhanti, killing a bodhisattva on the Definite Stage (niyatabhumi), killing an noble being on the path of training (i.e., not yet an arhant), robbing the sangha of means of livelihood, and destroying a stupa.

FIVE DEGENERATIONS (snyigs ma lnga)   (1) The degeneration of views due to the decline in the virtue of renunciants means wrong views. (2) The degeneration of disturbing emotions due to the decline in the virtue of householders means coarse-natured minds in which coarseness refers to strong and long-lasting kleshas. (3) The degeneration of times due to the decline in enjoyments means the decreasing Aeon of Strife. (4) The degeneration of life span due to the decline of the sustaining life force means a decreasing life span until finally reaching the length of ten years. (5) The degeneration of sentient beings means the decline of body due to inferior shape and lesser size, the decline of merit due to lesser power and splendor, the decline of mind due to lesser sharpness of intellect, power of recollection, and diligence. Thus, the degeneration of sentient beings in whom the three types of decline have come together means that their minds are difficult to tame.

FIVE DISTURBING EMOTIONS (nyon mongs pa lnga)   Anger, desire, delusion, pride, and envy.

FIVE FAMILIES (rigs lnga)   The five buddha families of tathagata, vajra, ratna, padma, and karma. They represent the innate qualities of our enlightened essence.

FIVE KAYAS (sku lnga)   In this book the five kayas or aspects of buddhahood are dharmakaya, sambhogakaya, nirmanakaya, essence kaya, and great bliss kaya. They are defined in the chapter "Vajrayana Mind Training."

FIVE KINDS OF OFFERINGS (nyer spyod lnga)   The desirable objects of the five senses.

FIVE PATHS (lam lnga)   The paths of accumulation, joining, seeing, cultivation, and no-learning. The five paths cover the entire process from beginning Dharma practice to complete enlightenment.

FIVE SUPERKNOWLEDGES (mngon shes lnga)   The capacities for performing miracles, divine sight, divine hearing, recollection of former lives, and cognition of the minds of others.

FIVE WISDOMS (ye shes lnga)   The dharmadhatu wisdom, mirrorlike wisdom, wisdom of equality, discriminating wisdom, and all-accomplishing wisdom.

FIXATION ('dzin pa)   The mental act of holding on to a material object, experience, concept, or set of philosophical ideas.

FIXATION ON CONCRETENESS (dngos 'dzin)   The habitual tendency to cling to self and outer things as being real, solid, and lasting.

FOCUS (dmigs pa)   A conceptual object held in mind or the act of apprehending such an object. The practice called "accumulation of merit" involves holding in mind and cultivating a virtuous focus, while the "accumulation of wisdom" is cultivated by sustaining awareness totally free from holding any conceptual focus or reference point whatsoever.

FORM KAYAS (gzugs sku)   The sambhogakaya and nirmanakaya that have perceptible form as opposed to the formless dharmakaya.

FORM REALM (gzugs khams; Skt. rupa-dhatu)   Seventeen samsaric heavenly abodes consisting of the threefold four dhyana realms and the five pure abodes. A subtle divine state of samsaric existence between the desire realm and the formless realm, where sense of smell, sense of taste, and sexual organs are absent. The beings there have bodies of light, long lives, and no painful sensations. Unwholesome mental factors such as attachment cannot arise.

FORMLESS REALM (gzugs med khams; Skt. arupya-dhatu)   The most subtle state of samsaric existence, without anything physical at all, lacking even mental pleasure. The abode of an unenlightened being who has practiced the four absorptions. Its beings dwell in unchanging equanimity for long durations of time, after which they again return to lower states within samsara.

FOUR ACTIVITIES (las bzhi)   Pacifying, increasing, magnetizing, and subjugating.

FOUR ASPECTS OF APPROACH AND ACCOMPLISHMENT (bsnyen sgrub kyi yan lag bzhi)   Approach, full approach, accomplishment, and great accomplishment. Four important aspects of Vajrayana practice, especially the recitation stage of yidam practice. These four aspects, however, can apply to any level of meaning within the tantras. Their traditional analogy is to invite the ruler of a country, to present him with gifts and make a specific request, to obtain his permission to carry out one's aim, and to use one's authority to accomplish the welfare of self and others. In the context of recitation practice, *approach* is to visualize the yidam deity with the mantra in its heart center, *full approach* is the spinning garland of mantra syllables that emanates light rays making offerings to all the buddhas in the ten directions, *accomplishment* is to receive their blessings that purify all one's obscurations, and *great accomplishment* transforms the world into the mandala of buddha-field, the beings into male and female deities, sounds into mantra, and all thoughts and emotions into a pure display of innate wakefulness.

FOUR CLASSES OF DAKINIS (mkha' 'gro sde bzhi) The dakinis of the
four families of vajra, ratna, padma, and karma. They are spiritual beings
who carry out the four activities of pacifying, increasing, magnetizing,
and subjugating.

FOUR DAILY ACTIVITIES (spyod lam bzhi) Walking, moving about,
lying down, and sitting.

FOUR EMPOWERMENTS (dbang bzhi) The empowerments of vase, secret,
wisdom-knowledge, and precious word. Padmasambhava says in the
Lamrim Yeshe Nyingpo:

> The vase empowerment which purifies the body and the nadis
> Is the seed of the vajra body and nirmanakaya.
> The secret empowerment which purifies the speech and the pranas
> Is the seed of the vajra speech and sambhogakaya.
> The phonya empowerment which purifies the mind and the
>   bindus
> Is the seed of the vajra mind and dharmakaya.
> The ultimate empowerment which purifies the habitual patterns of
>   the all-ground
> Is the seed of the vajra wisdom and svabhavikakaya.

FOUR IMMEASURABLES (tshad med bzhi) Compassion, love, joy, and
impartiality.

FOUR MAGICAL POWERS (rdzu 'phrul bzhi) In the general vehicles,
the four legs of miraculous action (rdzu 'phrul gyi rkang pa bzhi) are
mentioned as intention, determination, diligence, and discernment; four
causes for achieving the power of superknowledge. In Vajrayana, four
magical displays (cho 'phrul bzhi) are mentioned as being samadhi,
consecration, conferring empowerment, and making offerings.

FOUR MEANS OF MAGNETIZING (bsdu ba'i dngos po bzhi) Being
generous, uttering kind words, giving appropriate teachings, and keeping
consistency between words and actions. Padmasambhava says in the
Lamrim Yeshe Nyingpo:

> Having ripened your own being, gather followers through
>   generosity,
> Delight them with pleasing words, and comfort them by being
>   consistent.
> Through giving them counsel to meaningful conduct, establish
>   them temporarily and ultimately,
> In the full splendor of benefit and well-being.

FOUR PARAMITAS (phar phyin bzhi) The last four of the ten paramitas:
skillful means, strength, aspiration, and wisdom.

FOUR VIDYADHARA LEVELS (rig 'dzin rnam pa bzhi 'i go 'phang) The four stages of attainment of knowledge holders, masters of the four stages of the tantric path of mahayoga. The four vidyadhara levels are the full maturation, life mastery, mahamudra, and spontaneous presence (rnam smin, tshe dbang, phyag chen, lhun grub).

FOURFOLD SPHERES OF PERCEPTION (skye mched mu bzhi) Same as the four formless realms. The four unenlightened meditative states of dwelling on the thoughts: infinite space, infinite consciousness, nothing whatsoever, and neither presence nor absence of conception.

FREEDOMS AND RICHES (dal 'byor) The conditions for being able to practice the sacred Dharma in a human body.

FRUITION OF THE TWO KAYAS (sku gnyis kyi 'bras bu) The state of complete and perfect buddhahood comprised of dharmakaya and rupa-kaya, of which rupakaya, the form body, refers to both sambhogakaya and nirmanakaya.

FULL APPROACH (nye bar bsnyen pa) *See* Four aspects of approach and accomplishment.

GANACHAKRA (tshogs kyi 'khor lo). *See* Wheel of gathering.

GARUDA BIRD (bya khyung) A mythological bird, able to travel from one end of the universe to the other with a single movement of its wings. It is also said to hatch from the egg fully developed and ready to soar through the sky. In the Dzogchen teachings, the garuda symbolizes the inner accomplishment of a meditator for whom the spontaneously present qualities of the buddha nature become fully manifest at the moment of death; the attainment of buddhahood occurs simultaneously with leaving the physical body behind.

GATHERING ACCUMULATIONS (tshogs bsags pa) The virtuous prac-tices of perfecting the two accumulations of merit and wisdom.

GLORIOUS SAMYE AT RED ROCK (brag dmar dpal gyi bsam yas) The fabulous temple complex of Samye in central Tibet built by King Trisong Deutsen (790–844). The mountain slope behind Samye is of a bright red color.

GREAT ACCOMPLISHMENT (sgrub pa chen po) The fourth of the four aspects of approach and accomplishment.

GREAT ACCOMPLISHMENT PRACTICE (sgrub chen) A sadhana prac-tice undertaken by a group of people that goes on uninterruptedly for seven days.

GREAT BLISS KAYA (bde ba chen po'i sku; Skt, mahasukhakaya)

Among the five kayas, the uncompounded quality of changelessness.

GREAT PERFECTION (rdzogs pa chen po)   Same as *Dzogchen*. The third of the three inner tantras of the Nyingma School.

GREATER AND LESSER VEHICLES (theg pa che chung)   Mahayana and Hinayana. Mahayana includes the tantric vehicles. Hinayana is comprised of the teachings for shravakas and pratyekabuddhas. The connotation of "greater" or "lesser" refers to the scope of aspiration, the methods applied, and the depth of insight.

GURU (bla ma)   Spiritual teacher.

GURU, YIDAM AND DAKINI (bla ma yi dam mkha' 'gro)   The three roots of Vajrayana practice: the guru is the root of blessings, the yidam, the root of accomplishments, and the dakini, the root of activities.

HABITUAL TENDENCIES (bag chags)   Subtle inclinations imprinted in the all-ground consciousness.

HEARING LINEAGE (nyan brgyud)   The lineage of oral teachings from master to disciple.

HEAT (drod)   The first of the four aspects of ascertainment on the path of joining. Getting close to the flamelike wisdom of the path of seeing by possessing concentration concurrent with discriminating knowledge.

HERETICAL PEOPLE (mu stegs pa)   People holding wrong views, that there is no consequence from negative actions, no past or future lives, no result from practicing the path, and so forth.

HIGHER OR LOWER VEHICLES (theg pa mtho dman)   Same as "greater and lesser vehicles."

HIGHER PERCEPTIONS (mngon par shes pa)   *See* Superknowledge.

HIGHER REALMS (mtho ris)   The three higher realms of humans, demigods, and gods.

HINAYANA (theg pa dman pa)   The vehicles focused on contemplation of the four noble truths and the twelve links of dependent origination for the sake of individual liberation.

HUNGRY GHOSTS (yid dvags)   One of the six classes of sentient beings. Such beings are tormented by their own impure karmic perception, causing them to suffer tremendously from craving, hunger, and thirst.

INDIVIDUAL LIBERATION (so sor thar pa; Skt. pratimoksha)   The seven sets of precepts for ordained and lay people according to the vinaya of Hinayana. The vows of laymen and laywomen; the vows of male and female novices; additional vows taken by probational nuns as a step toward becoming full nuns; the discipline of the full nun (bhikshuni); that of the full monk (bhikshu). There are eight types when including fasting vows, taken for one day only. The precepts of individual liberation are the basic code of morality that are the common foundation for all Buddhist practice.

INDIVIDUAL SELF (gang zag gi bdag) The mistaken idea that there exists an "I" that is an independent, singular, and permanent entity.

INDRA (brgya byin) The chief god in the realm of desire. He resides on the summit of Mount Sumeru in the Palace of Complete Victory and is also known as Shakra, the ruler of the devas.

JAMBUDVIPA (dzam bu gling) The continent situated to the south of Mount Sumeru, the center of the world in Buddhist cosmology.

KARMIC CONTINUITY OF FORMER PRACTICE (sngon sbyangs kyi las 'phro) The continuity of Dharma practice from the previous life.

KAYA (sku) *Body* in the sense of a body or embodiment of numerous qualities.

KILAYA (phur ba) Sacred dagger used in tantric rituals.

KLESHAS (nyon mongs pa) Same as "disturbing emotions."

KNOWING ONE THAT FREES ALL (gcig shes kun grol) Insight into one's buddha nature, the basic state within all thoughts and emotions, will automatically liberate fixation on those occurrences.

KNOWLEDGE (shes rab) *See* Means and knowledge.

LADY TSOGYAL (jo mo mtsho rgyal) Also known as Khandro Yeshe Tsogyal, she was the close disciple of Guru Rinpoche, and compiled the major part of his teachings.

LIBERATION (thar pa) Emancipation from samsaric existence.

LORD OF THE FAMILY (rigs kyi bdag po) The chief buddha of the family to which one's particular yidam deity belongs. For example, Avalokiteshvara's crown buddha is Amitabha.

LOWER PHILOSOPHICAL SCHOOLS (grub mtha' dman pa) The two main Hinayana schools, Vaibhashika and Sautrantika. Compared to Mahayana they are called lower in that they fail to establish the emptiness of all phenomena.

LOWER REALMS (ngan song) The three abodes of hell beings, hungry ghosts, and animals.

LOWER VEHICLES (theg pa 'og ma)   Compared to Vajrayana, the lower vehicles are those of shravakas, pratyekabuddhas, and bodhisattvas.

LUMINOSITY ('od gsal)   Literally "free from the darkness of unknowing and endowed with the ability to cognize." The two aspects are empty luminosity, like a clear open sky, and manifest luminosity, such as five-colored lights, images, and so forth. Luminosity is the uncompounded nature present throughout all of samsara and nirvana.

LUMINOUS DHARMATA (chos nyid 'od gsal)   The innate wakefulness that is the nature of mind of all sentient beings.

MAGICAL SAMADHI (sgyu ma lta bu'i ting nge 'dzin)   The second of the three samadhis, the nature of which is luminosity and compassion, spontaneous like the light of the sun shining in the sky. *See also* Three samadhis.

MAHADEVA (lha chen)   A form of Shiva.

MAHAMUDRA (phyag rgya chen po)   In the context of this book, *mahamudra* refers either to the supreme attainment of mahamudra, which is synonymous with complete enlightenment, or to the mahamudra form of the yidam deity, mentioned below.

MAHAMUDRA FORM OF THE YIDAM DEITY (yidam lha'i phyag chen kyi lus)   The attainment, chiefly through Mahayoga Tantra, of the illusory wisdom body on the vidyadhara level of mahamudra, which corresponds to the path of cultivation. It is a divine form of a deity endowed with the complete major and minor marks and through which the yogi is able to benefit beings in an extent that is equal to the sambhogakaya.

MAHANIRVANA (mya ngan las 'das pa chen po)   The state of final buddhahood that dwells neither in samsaric existence nor in the passive nirvana of an arhant.

MAHASANDHI (Skt., rdzogs pa chen po)   *See* Dzogchen.

MAHAYANA (theg pa chen po)   The vehicle of bodhisattvas striving for perfect enlightenment for the sake of liberating all sentient beings. Mahayana has two aspects: sutra, emphasizing the extensive teachings, and mantra, emphasizing the profound. For a detailed explanation of sutrayana, see Maitreya's *Abhisamayalamkara* or Gampopa's *The Jewel Ornament of Liberation* by sGam.po.pa, trans. Herbert V. Guenther (Boston: Shambhala Publications, 1986).

MAHAYANA TEACHINGS (theg pa chen po'i chos)   The Buddha's teachings comprised of the second and third turning of the wheel of

Dharma as well as the commentaries upon them by the great scholars of India and Tibet.

MAHESHVARA (dbang phyug chen po)   One of the chief Hindu divinities.

MAJOR AND MINOR MARKS (mtshan dpe)   The thirty-two major and eighty minor marks of excellence that characterize the perfect physical form of a nirmanakaya or sambhogakaya buddha. A universal ruler is also said to possess a resemblance to these marks.

MANDALA (dkyil 'khor)   Literally means "center and surrounding." Usually a deity along with its surrounding environment. Mandala is a symbolic representation of a tantric deity's realm of existence, an entire universe visualized as an offering, and also the arrangement of offerings in tantric ritual.

MANTRA (sngags)   (1) A synonym for Vajrayana. (2) A particular combination of sounds symbolizing and communicating the nature of a deity, which leads to purification and realization; for example, OM MANI PADME HUNG. There are chiefly three types: guhya mantra, vidya mantra, and dharani mantra.

MANTRA AND PHILOSOPHY. *Mantra* means Vajrayana, while the vehicle of philosophy includes both Hinayana and Mahayana.

MANTRADHARA (sngags 'chang)   An adept of tantric rituals.

MARA (bdud)   Demon or demonic influence that creates obstacles for practice and enlightenment. Mythologically said to dwell in the highest abode in the realm of desire, Mara is a master of illusion who attempted to prevent the Buddha from attaining enlightenment at Bodh Gaya. For the Dharma practitioner, Mara symbolizes one's own ego-clinging and preoccupation with the eight worldly concerns.

MARA OF MERITORIOUS ACTION (bsod nams kyi las kyi bdud)   The seductive tendency to aim one's spiritual practice toward selfish ends. Virtuous deeds that are not embraced by renunciation or bodhicitta.

MASTER (bla ma, slob dpon)   Title given to spiritual teachers and learned scholars. In this book, *master* often refers to Guru Rinpoche.

MEANS (thabs; Skt. upaya)   The methods or skillful means that are the practical application of the Buddhist teachings. Can also refer to the seventh of the ten paramitas.

MEANS AND KNOWLEDGE (thabs dang shes rab; Skt. upaya and prajna)   Buddhahood is attained by uniting means and knowledge; in Mahayana, they are compassion and emptiness, relative and ultimate bodhicitta. In Vajrayana, means and knowledge are the stages of development and completion. According to the Kagyu schools, *means* refers specifically to the "path of means," the six doctrines of Naropa, and knowledge to the "path of liberation," the actual practice of mahamudra. According to Dzogchen, *knowledge* is the view of primordial purity, the trekcho practice of realizing the heart of enlightenment in the present moment, while *means* is the meditation of spontaneous presence, the thogal practice of exhausting defilements and fixation through which the rainbow body is realized within one lifetime.

MEDITATOR (sgom chen)   A person all of whose time is spent on meditation practice, often in mountain retreats. The special connotation is a full-time practitioner of ordinary mind or unfabricated naturalness.

MERIT (bsod nams)   The positive karmic result from virtuous actions.

MIDDLE WAY (dbu ma; Skt. madhyamaka)   The highest of the four Buddhist schools of philosophy. The Middle Way means not holding any extreme views, especially those of eternalism or nihilism.

MIND-ESSENCE (sems nyid)   The nature of one's mind, which is taught to be identical with the essence of all enlightened beings, the sugatagarbha. It should be distinguished from *mind* (sems), which refers to ordinary discursive thinking based on ignorance of the nature of thought.

MONKHA SENGA DZONG.   A cave situated to the east of Bumthang in Bhutan that was used by Padmasambhava and later by Yeshe Tsogyal as a sacred place for sadhana.

MOUNT SUMERU (ri rab lhun po)   The mythological giant mountain at the center of the world system, where the two lowest classes of gods of the desire realm live. It is surrounded by chains of lesser mountains, lakes, continents, and oceans and is said to rise eighty-four thousand leagues above sea level.

NAGA (klu)   Powerful, long-lived, serpentlike beings who inhabit bodies of water and often guard great treasure. They belong half to the animal realm and half to the god realm. They generally live in the form of snakes, but many can change into human form and they are often depicted as human from the waist up, with a serpent's tail below. They are supposed to control the weather, especially rain.

NAMO (phyag 'tshal lo)   Homage or salutation.

NIHILISM (chad lta)   Literally, "the view of discontinuance." The extreme view of nothingness: no rebirth or karmic effects, and the nonexistence of a mind after death.

NINE GRADUAL VEHICLES (theg pa rim pa dgu)   Shravaka, pratyekabuddha, bodhisattva, kriya, upa, yoga, maha, anu, and ati.

NIRMANAKAYA (sprul sku)   Emanation body. The third of the three kayas. The aspect of enlightenment that tames, and can be perceived by, ordinary beings.

NIRMANAKAYA MASTER (slob dpon sprul pa'i sku) A respectful way of addressing Guru Rinpoche showing that he is a manifestation of an enlightened being.

NIRVANA (mya ngan las 'das pa) The extinguishing of the causes for samsaric existence. The lesser nirvana refers to the liberation from cyclic existence attained by a Hinayana practitioner. When referring to a buddha, nirvana is the great nondwelling state of enlightenment that falls neither into the extreme of samsaric existence nor into the passive state of cessation attained by an arhant.

NOBLE BEINGS (skyes mchog) Great masters, bodhisattvas, or arhants, who have attained the path of seeing, the third of the five paths.

NOBLE SANGHA ('phags pa'i dge 'dun) The congregation of practitioners who have attained the path of seeing, the third of the five paths.

NON-BUDDHISTS (phyi pa, mu stegs pa; Skt. tirthika) Teachers of philosophy adhering to the extreme views of eternalism or nihilism, especially a Hindu, Jain, or lokyata (materialist).

NONARISING (skye ba med pa) In the aspect of ultimate truth, all phenomena are devoid of an independent, concrete identity and have therefore no basis for such attributes as arising, dwelling, or ceasing.

NONCONCEPTUAL SELF-COGNIZANCE (rtog med rang gsal) The basic state of mind that is pointed out by the root guru, free from thoughts and yet naturally cognizing whatever is present.

NONCONCEPTUALIZATION OF THE THREE SPHERES ('khor gsum dmigs med) Not holding on to the concepts of subject, object, and action.

NONDHARMIC (chos min) Any attribute or action that is in conflict with the Dharma, especially the eight worldly concerns.

NONMEDITATION (sgom med) The state of not holding on to an object meditated upon nor to a subject who meditates. Also refers to the fourth stage of mahamudra, in which nothing further needs to be meditated upon or cultivated.

NONTHOUGHT (mi rtog) A state in which conceptual thinking is absent. It can refer to nonconceptual wakefulness, but usually it is one of the three temporary meditation experiences: bliss, clarity, and nonthought.

OBSCURATION OF DUALISTIC KNOWLEDGE (shes bya'i sgrib

pa) The subtle obscuration of holding on to the concepts of subject, object, and action.

OBSCURATIONS (sgrib pa) The veils that cover one's direct perception of the nature of mind. In the general Buddhist teachings several types are mentioned: the obscuration of karma preventing one from entering the path of enlightenment, the obscuration of disturbing emotions preventing progress along the path, the obscuration of habitual tendencies preventing the vanishing of confusion, and the final obscuration of dualistic knowledge preventing the full attainment of buddhahood.

OMNISCIENCE (rnam mkhyen, thams cad mkhyen pa) Same as complete enlightenment or buddhahood.

OMNISCIENT ONES (thams cad mkhyen pa) As opposed to the scholastic tradition, the oral instructions of the practice lineage are concise and pithy so they can always be kept in mind; they are practical and to the point so they are effective means to deal directly with the practices of purifying one's obscurations and gathering the two accumulations.

ORDINARINESS (tha mal) The state of mind of an ordinary person that is not embraced by renunciation or insight into egolessness nor by the bodhicitta aspiration, pure perception, or recognition of the nature of mind. In that state one's thoughts and emotions will arise unchallenged and automatically accumulate the karma for further samsaric existence.

ORDINARY MIND (tha mal gyi shes pa) Mind in the state of unfabricated naturalness. A key word in vajrayana practice.

ORDINARY PERCEPTION (tha mal gyi snang ba) The way an ordinary person experiences. *See also* Ordinariness.

ORGYEN (o rgyen; Skt. Uddiyana) Also known as Uddiyana or Odiyan, it is the home of many dakinis, and the birth place of Padmasambhava; thought to be located in the Swat valley northwest of India, which borders on modern Afghanistan. In prehistoric times, the great demon of ego-clinging was subdued and liberated by Hayagriva and Vajra Yogini. As his body fell to the ground, the heart landed in the country of Uddiyana, forming the special auspicious coincidence for the spread of the Vajrayana teachings.

OUTER AND INNER VEHICLES (phyi nang gi theg pa) Same as higher and lower vehicles. Hinayana and Mahayana.

PADMAKARA (pad ma 'byung gnas) "Lotus-born." Same as Guru Rinpoche. The names Padmakara and Padmasambhava are used interchangeably in Tibetan literature, sometimes in the Tibetan version, sometimes in Sanskrit.

PARAMITA (pha rol tu phyin pa) "Reaching the other shore." Transcending concepts of subject, object, and action. *See also* Six paramitas, Ten paramitas.

PATH OF ACCUMULATION (tshogs lam) The first of the five paths, which forms the foundation for the journey toward liberation and involves gathering a vast accumulation of merit dedicated toward this attainment. On this path one gains an intellectual and conceptual understanding of egolessness through learning and reflection. By means of cultivating the four applications of mindfulness, the four right endeavors, and the four legs of miraculous action, one succeeds in eliminating the gross defilements that cause samsaric suffering and in attaining the virtuous qualities of the superknowledges and the "samadhi of the stream of Dharma" leading to the path of accumulation.

PATH OF CONSUMMATION (thar phyin pa'i lam) The fifth of the five paths and the state of complete and perfect enlightenment.

PATH OF CULTIVATION (sgom lam) The fourth of the five paths on which one cultivates and trains in the higher practices of a bodhisattva, especially the eight aspects of the path of noble beings.

PATH OF JOINING (sbyor lam) The second of the five paths, on which one grows closer to and joins with the realization of the truth of reality.

PATH OF SEEING (mthong lam) The third of the five paths, which is the attainment of the first bhumi, liberation from samsara, and realization of the truth of reality.

PATHS (lam) The five paths or stages on the way to enlightenment: the paths of accumulation, joining, seeing, cultivation, and no more learning. They can be explained differently according to each of the three vehicles.

PATHS AND BHUMIS (sa lam) The five paths and the ten bodhisattva levels.

PEACEFUL AND WRATHFUL BUDDHAS (zhi khro) The forty-two peaceful buddhas: Samantabhadra and Samantabhadri, the five male and female buddhas, the eight male and female bodhisattvas, the six munis, and the four male and female gatekeepers; the fifty-eight wrathful buddhas: the five male and female herukas, the eight yoginis, the eight tramen goddesses, the four female gatekeepers, the twenty-eight shvaris. For further details see *The Tibetan Book of the Dead: Hearing through Liberation in the Bardo,* trans. Francesca Fremantle & Chögyam Trungpa (Boston: Shambhala Publications, 1987).

PERCEPTION-SPHERES (skye mched) Refers here to the states of mind of the four formless realms. *See also* Fourfold spheres of perception.

PHENOMENA (chos, snang ba) Anything that can be experienced, thought of, or known.

PHILOSOPHICAL SCHOOLS (grub mtha') The four Buddhist schools of thought are: Vaibhashika, Sautrantika, Cittamatra, and Madhyamaka. The former two are Hinayana and the latter two Mahayana.

PHILOSOPHICAL VEHICLE (mtshan nyid kyi theg pa) A collective name for Hinayana and Mahayana.

PRAJNAPARAMITA (shes rab kyi pha rol tu phyin pa) Transcendent knowledge. The Mahayana teachings on insight into emptiness, transcending the fixation of subject, object, and action. Associated with the second turning of the Wheel of Dharma.

PRANA (Skt., rlung) The energy currents in the body.

PRANA-MIND (rlung sems) *Prana* here is the "wind of karma" and *mind* is the dualistic consciousness of an unenlightened being. The two are closely related.

PRATYEKABUDDHA (rang rgyal, rang sangs rgyas) Solitarily enlightened one. A Hinayana arhant who attains nirvana chiefly through contemplation on the twelve links of dependent origination in reverse order, without needing teachings in that lifetime, but lacks the complete realization of a buddha and so cannot benefit limitless sentient beings as a buddha does.

PRECIOUS MIND OF ENLIGHTENMENT (byang chub kyi sems rin po che) *See* Bodhicitta.

PRECIOUS ONES (dkon mchog) Same as the Three Jewels. *See also* Three Precious Ones. For further details of their qualities, see *Buddha Nature* by Thrangu Rinpoche (Rangjung Yeshe Publications, 1988).

PRINCESS OF KHARCHEN (mkhar chen bza') Same as Yeshe Tsogyal.

PURE PERCEPTION (dag snang) Regarding the environment as a buddha-field, self and others as deities, sounds as mantras, and thoughts as wisdom.

PURIFYING THE OBSCURATIONS (sgrib sbyong) The spiritual practices of clearing away what obscures the sugatagarbha; for example, the meditation and recitation of vajrasattva according to the special preliminaries.

QUALIFIED MASTER (bla ma mtshan nyid dang ldan pa) Someone with the correct view and genuine compassion. For details see Longchempa, *Kindly Bent to Ease Us*, Vol. I, trans. Herbert V. Guenther (London: Dharma Publishing).

RAINBOW BODY ('ja' lus) At the time of death of a practitioner who has reached the exhaustion of all grasping and fixation through the

Dzogchen practice of thogal, the five gross elements that form the physical body dissolve back into their essences, five-colored light. Sometimes only the hair and the nails are left behind.

RAKSHAS (srin po) An evil being or demon.

RASAYANA (bcud len) *See* Extracting essences.

REALM OF FORM (gzugs kyi khams) *See* Form realm.

RECITATION (bzlas pa) The part of sadhana practice that covers recitation of a mantra.

RESULTANT SYSTEM OF SECRET MANTRA ('bras bu gsang sngags) The Vajrayana system of taking the fruition as the path by regarding buddhahood as inherently present and the path as the act of uncovering one's basic state. This is different from the "causal philosophical vehicles" of Mahayana and Hinayana that regard the path as that which leads to and produces the state of buddhahood. Ultimately, these two approaches are not in conflict. *See also* Secret Mantra.

ROOTS OF VIRTUE (dge ba'i rtsa ba) Good deeds.

RUDRAS (ru dra) (1) A type of unruly half-god, half-demon. (2) The demon of ego-clinging.

RUPAKAYA (gzugs kyi sku) Form body. A collective term for both sambhogakaya and nirmanakaya.

SADHANA (sgrub thabs) Means of accomplishment. Tantric liturgy and procedure for practice usually emphasizing the development stage.

SAHA (Skt., mi mjed) The name of our present world system. It means "enduring" because the sentient beings here endure unbearable suffering.

SAMADHI (ting nge 'dzin) Adhering to continuity or evenness. Usually translated as concentration or meditative absorption.

SAMADHI OF SUCHNESS (de bzhin nyid kyi ting nge 'dzin) The first of the three samadhis.

SAMANTABHADRA (kun tu bzang po) The Ever-Excellent One. (1) The primordial dharmakaya buddha. (2) The bodhisattva Samantabhadra used as the example for the perfection of increasing an offering infinitely.

SAMAYA (dam tshig) (1) The sacred pledge, precepts, or commitment of Vajrayana practice. Many details exist, but the samayas essentially consist of, outwardly, maintaining harmonious relationships with the vajra master and one's Dharma friends and, inwardly, not straying from the continuity of the practice. (2) At the end of a chapter, the single word *samaya* is an oath that what has been stated is true.

SAMAYA BEING (dam tshig sems dpa', dam tshig pa) The deity visualized by oneself.

SAMBHOGAKAYA (longs spyod rdzogs pa'i sku)   The body of perfect enjoyment. Of the five kayas of fruition, this is the semi-manifest form of the buddhas endowed with the five perfections of perfect teacher, retinue, place, teaching, and time, which is perceptible only to bodhisattvas on the ten bhumis.

SAMSARA ('khor ba)   Cyclic existence, vicious circle, or round of birth and death and rebirth within the six realms of existence, characterized by suffering, impermanence, and ignorance. The state of ordinary sentient beings fettered by ignorance and dualistic perception, karma, and disturbing emotions. Ordinary reality: an endless cycle of frustration and suffering generated as the result of karma.

SAMSARIC EXISTENCE ('khor ba, srid pa)   *See* Samsara.

SAMYE (bsam yas)   The temple built by King Trisong Deutsen and consecrated by Guru Rinpoche. It is situated in central Tibet close to Lhasa. *See also* Glorious Samye at Red Rock.

SANGHA (dge 'dun)   The community or congregation of practitioners. In "taking refuge in the Noble Sangha," it means those who have achieved the path of seeing among the five paths and therefore are liberated from samsara.

SECRET MANTRA (gsang sngags; Skt. Guhyamantra)   Synonymous with Vajrayana or tantric teachings. *Guhya* means secret, both concealed and self-secret. *Mantra* in this context means eminent, excellent, or praiseworthy.

SELF OF PHENOMENA (chos kyi bdag)   An independent entity or inherently existent identity in phenomena.

SELF OF THE INDIVIDUAL (gang zag gi bdag)   *See* Individual self.

SELF-ENTITY (rang bzhin)   An inherently existent and independent entity of the individual self or of phenomena.

SELF-NATURE (rang bzhin)   An inherently existent and independent substance of the individual self or of phenomena. Something that can serve as a valid basis for individual attributes.

SELFLESSNESS (bdag med)   The innate absence of a self-entity in the individual person as well as in matter and mind.

SENTIENT BEING (sems can)   Any living being in one of the six realms who has not attained liberation.

SEVEN BRANCHES (yan lag bdun pa)   The seven-branch practice of prostrating to the Three Jewels, confessing negative actions, making offerings, rejoicing in the virtue of others, requesting to turn the wheel of Dharma, beseeching to not pass into nirvana, and dedicating the merit to the enlightenment of all sentient beings.

SEVEN POINTS OF MEDITATION POSTURE (sgom tshul gyi gnad bdun) The legs in cross-legged position, with the spine straight, the shoulders extended, the neck slightly bent, the hands in the gesture of equanimity, the tip of tongue touching the palate, and the gaze placed in the direction of the nose.

SEVEN PURE ASPECTS (bdun rnam dag) Same as the seven branches.

SEVEN PURITIES (dag pa bdun) Same as the seven branches.

SHAKYAMUNI (sha kya thub pa) The sage of the Shakyas, Buddha Shakyamuni, our historical buddha.

SHAMATHA (zhi gnas) Calm abiding or remaining in quiescence after thought activity has subsided; or, the meditative practice of calming the mind in order to rest free from the disturbance of thought.

SHRAVAKA (nyan thos) Hearer or listener. Hinayana practitioner of the first set of teachings given by the Buddha, which presents the four noble truths, who realizes the suffering inherent in samsara and focuses on understanding that there is no independent self. By conquering disturbing emotions, he liberates himself, attaining first the stage of stream enterer on the path of seeing, followed by the stage of once-returner who will be reborn only one more time, and the stage of nonreturner who will no longer be reborn into samsara. The final goal is to become an arhant.

SHRAVAKA'S STATE OF CESSATION (zhi gnas 'gog pa) In the context of Mahayana or Vajrayana practice, this state is used in a derogatory sense and is renowned as a severe sidetrack from the path of the enlightenment of the buddhas. The mistake comes from regarding meditation practice as being the act of cultivating and fixating on a state in which sensations and thoughts are absent.

SHUNYATA MANTRA (shu nya ta'i sngags) The mantra OM SVABHAVA SHUDDHO SARVA DHARMA SVABHAVA SHUDDHO 'HAM.

SIDDHA (grub thob, grub pa) Perfected one, realized one, adept who has attained siddhi.

SIDDHI (dngos grub) Accomplishment. The attainment resulting from Dharma practice, usually referring to the supreme siddhi of complete enlightenment. It can also mean the common siddhis, eight mundane accomplishments such as clairvoyance, clairaudiance, flying in the sky, becoming invisible, everlasting youth, or powers of transmutation; the ability to control the body and the external world. The most eminent attainments on the path are, however, renunciation, compassion, unshakable faith, and realization of the correct view.

SIDDHI OF MAHAMUDRA (phyag rgya chen po'i dngos grub) Same as enlightenment. In the context of Mahayoga Tantra, it can also refer to the attainment of the third vidyadhara level, in which *mahamudra* means the sublime body of the yidam deity.

SINGLE CIRCLE OF DHARMAKAYA (chos sku thig le nyag cig) All buddhas are one in the all-encompassing space of dharmakaya, which is round in the sense of being beyond the "corners" of thought constructs.

SIX CLASSES OF BEINGS ('gro ba rigs drug) Gods, demigods, human beings, animals, hungry ghosts, and hell beings.

SIX PARAMITAS (phar phyin drug) The six transcendent actions of generosity, discipline, patience, diligence, concentration, and discriminating knowledge.

SIX SENSE FACULTIES (dbang po drug) The five senses and the mental faculty.

SIX SUPERKNOWLEDGES The capacities for performing miracles, divine sight, divine hearing, recollection of former lives, cognition of the minds of others, and the cognition of the exhaustion of defilements.

SUBSTANCE OF ACCOMPLISHMENT (dngos grub kyi rdzas) The shrine articles, such as amrita and torma, of which a small portion is partaken of on the morning of the last day of a retreat practice.

SUCHNESS (de bzhin nyid; Skt. tattva) Synonym for emptiness or the nature of things, dharmata, it can also be used to describe the unity of dependent origination and emptiness.

SUGATA (bde bar gshegs pa) Blissfully gone. Same as a buddha.

SUGATA-ESSENCE (bde gshegs snying po) Another word for buddha nature, the enlightened essence inherent in sentient beings.

SUMMIT (rtse mo) One of the four aspects of ascertainment on the path of joining.

SUPERKNOWLEDGE (mngon par shes pa) Usually refers to the six higher perceptions, including clairvoyance, knowledge of other's minds, and so forth. *See also* Six superknowledges.

SUPREME AND COMMON ACCOMPLISHMENTS *See* Siddhis.

SUPREME ATTAINMENT OF MAHAMUDRA (phyag rgya chen po mchog gi dngos grub) (1) Supreme enlightenment. (2) The third of the four vidyadhara levels.

SUPREME ENLIGHTENMENT (byang chub mchog, byang chub snying po) Same as buddhahood.

SUPREME MUNDANE ATTRIBUTE ('jig rten chos mchog) The fourth of the four aspects of ascertainment on the path of joining. The highest spiritual attainment within samsaric existence.

SUTRA (mdo) Discourse or teaching by the Buddha. Also refers to all the causal teachings that regard the path as the cause of enlightenment. *Compare with* Mantra.

TAKING REFUGE (skyabs 'gro) Placing one's trust in the Three Jewels.

TANTRA (rgyud) The Vajrayana teachings given by the Buddha in his sambhogakaya form. Literally "continuity," tantra means the buddha nature, the "tantra of the expressed meaning." Generally, the extraordinary tantric scriptures that are exalted above the sutras, the "tantra of the expressing words." Can also refer to all the resultant teachings that take the result as the path as a whole.

TANTRIC PRACTITIONER (sngags pa) A person who has received empowerment, continues the sadhana practice, and keeps the commitments.

TANTRIC SAMAYAS OF THE VIDYADHARAS (rig 'dzin sngags kyi dam tshig) The commitments of a Vajrayana practitioner.

TANTRIKA (sngags pa) *See* Tantric practitioner.

TATHAGATAS AND THEIR SONS (de gshegs sras bcas) The buddhas who have gone *(gata)* to the state of dharmata suchness *(tatha)*. Their sons are the bodhisattvas on the ten bhumis.

TEN BHUMIS (sa bcu) The ten levels of a noble bodhisattva's development into a fully enlightened buddha. On each stage more subtle defilements are purified and a further degree of enlightened qualities is manifested: the Joyous, the Stainless, the Radiant, the Brilliant, the Hard to Conquer, the Realized, the Reaching Far, the Unshakable, the Good Intelligence, and the Cloud of Dharma.

TEN NONVIRTUES (mi dge ba bcu) The physical misdeeds are killing, taking what is not given, and engaging in sexual misconduct. The verbal misdeeds are lying, uttering divisive talk, harsh words, and gossiping. The mental misdeeds are harboring covetousness, ill will, and wrong views.

TEN PARAMITAS (phar phyin bcu) The six paramitas in addition to means, strength, aspiration, and wisdom.

TEN VIRTUOUS ACTIONS (dge ba bcu) Generally, to refrain from the above ten unvirtuous actions. In particular, to engage in their opposites; for example, to save life, be generous, and so forth.

TERMA (gter ma) Treasure. The transmission through concealed treasures, hidden, mainly by Guru Rinpoche and Yeshe Tsogyal, to be revealed at the proper time by a terton, a treasure revealer for the benefit of future disciples.

TERTON (gter ston)   A revealer of hidden treasures, concealed mainly by Padmasambhava and Yeshe Tsogyal.

THATNESS (de bzhin nyid)   The nature of phenomena and mind.

THOGAL (thod rgal)   Direct crossing or passing above. Dzogchen, mahasandhi, has two main sections: trekcho and thogal. The former emphasizes primordial purity (ka dag) and the latter spontaneous presence (lhun grub).

THREE FAMILIES (rigs gsum)   Vajra, padma, and tathagata. When referring to the "lords of the three families," they are Manjushri, Avalokiteshvara, and Vajrapani.

THREE FIELDS OF OBJECTS (yul gsum)   The form of the deity appearing as either a perceptual object, as a mental object, or in the experience of the senses by someone else (snang yul, dbang yul, yid kyi yul).

THREE JEWELS (dkon mchog gsum)   The Precious Buddha, the Precious Dharma, and the Precious Sangha.

THREE KAYAS (sku gsum)   Dharmakaya, sambhogakaya, and nirmanakaya. The three kayas as ground are essence, nature, and expression; as path they are bliss, clarity, and nonthought; and as fruition they are the three kayas of buddhahood.

THREE KAYAS OF FRUITION ('bras bu'i sku gsum)   The dharmakaya is free from elaborate constructs and endowed with twenty-one sets of enlightened qualities. Sambhogakaya is of the nature of light and endowed with the perfect major and minor marks perceptible only to bodhisattvas on the bhumis. The nirmanakaya manifests in forms perceptible to both pure and impure beings.

THREE LEVELS OF ENLIGHTENMENT (byang chub gsum)   The attainment of the nirvana of an arhant, pratyekabuddha, and of a fully perfected buddha.

THREE LEVELS OF EXISTENCE (srid pa gsum)   Usually the same as the three realms.

THREE LOWER REALMS (ngan song gsum)   The worlds of hell beings, hungry ghosts, and animals.

THREE POISONS (dug gsum)   Desire, anger, and delusion.

THREE PRECIOUS ONES (dkon mchog gsum)   The Precious Buddha, Dharma, and Sangha.

THREE REALMS (khams gsum)   The samsaric realms of desire, form and formlessness.

THREE ROOTS (rtsa ba gsum)   Guru, yidam, and dakini. The guru is the root of blessings, the yidam of accomplishment, and the dakini of activity.

THREE SAMADHIS (ting nge 'dzin gsum) The samadhi of suchness, of illumination, and of the seed syllable. The samadhi of suchness is to rest in the composure of the innate emptiness of all phenomena, as pointed out by one's root master, or simply to imagine that all things are empty like space. The samadhi of illumination is to let natural compassion manifest like sunlight illuminating the sky, or simply to generate compassion for all the beings who fail to realize the nature of things. The samadhi of the seed syllable is the innate unity of emptiness and compassion manifesting in the form of a syllable that is the "seed" or source from which the deity and the entire mandala will appear during the practice. These three samadhis are the indispensable framework for the development stage of vajrayana practice. In his *Lamrim Yeshe Nyingpo,* Padmasambhava says:

> The main part begins with the profound and vast samadhis
> Which purify the manner of death, bardo, and rebirth:
> The great emptiness space of suchness is pure like the sky.
> Rest evenly in this space of the undivided two truths.
> Emanate the magic of compassion, an all-illuminating cloud of
>   awareness,
> Filling the space, radiant yet without fixation.
> The single mudra in the manner of a subtle syllable
> Is the causal seed which produces everything.
> Keep this changeless wisdom essence, manifest in space,
> One-pointedly in mind and bring its vivid presence to perfection.

THREE SPHERES OF CONCEPTS ('khor gsum gyi dmigs pa) Subject, object, and action.

THREE TYPES OF KNOWLEDGE (shes rab gsum) The understanding and insight resulting from learning, reflection, and meditation practice.

THREEFOLD VOWS (sdom pa gsum) The Hinayana vows of individual liberation, the Mahayana trainings of a bodhisattva, and the Vajrayana samayas of a vidyadhara.

TORMA (gtor ma) An implement used in tantric ceremonies. Can also refer to a food offering to Dharmapalas or unfortunate spirits.

TOTAL PURITY OF THE THREE CONCEPTS ('khor gsum rnam dag) Absence of fixation on subject, object, and action.

TRAMENMA (phra men) Goddesses with human bodies and animal heads. *Tramen* means hybrid or alloy.

TRANSITORY COLLECTION ('jig tshogs) Refers to the continuity of the five aggregates.

TREKCHO (khregs chod) "Cutting through" the stream of delusion, the thoughts of the three times by revealing naked awareness devoid of dualistic fixation. To recognize this view through the oral instructions of one's master and to sustain it uninterruptedly throughout all aspects of life is the very essence of Dzogchen practice.

TRISONG DEUTSEN (khri srong de'u btsan)   790–844. The second great Dharma king of Tibet, who invited Guru Rinpoche, Shantarakshita, Vimalamitra, and many other Buddhist teachers, including Jinamitra and Danashila, to Tibet. He built Samye, the great monastery and teaching center modeled after Odantapuri, and established Buddhism as the state religion of Tibet. During his reign the first monks were ordained. Panditas and lotsawas translated many texts, and large numbers of practice centers were established.

TRUE MEANING (nges don)   The definitive meaning as opposed to the expedient or relative meaning. The teachings of Prajnaparamita and the Middle Way. In his *Treasury of Knowledge*, Jamgon Kongtrul the Great defines the true, definitive meaning in the following way: The topics taught to exceptional disciples that the nature of all phenomena is profound emptiness devoid of constructs such as arising and ceasing, and that the innate real condition of things is by nature luminous wakefulness and lies beyond words, thoughts, and description. Moreover, it is the words of the Buddha expounding this meaning as well as the commentaries upon them.

TRULY HIGH (mngon mtho)   Refers to a rebirth in the three higher realms within samsara: humans, demigods, and gods.

TSA-TSA (tshva tshva)   A small clay image of a buddha stamped from a mold.

TURNING THE WHEEL OF DHARMA (chos kyi 'khor lo skor ba)   Figurative expression for giving Dharma teachings.

TWELVE SENSE-BASES (skye mched bcu gnyis)   The five senses and the mental faculty, and the five sense objects and mental objects.

TWO ACCUMULATIONS (tshogs gnyis)   The accumulation of merit with concepts and of wisdom beyond concepts.

TWOFOLD SELFLESSNESS (bdag med gnyis)   The inherent absence of a self-entity in the individual person as well as in all phenomena.

TWOFOLD SIDDHIS (dngos grub rnam gnyis)   See supreme and common siddhis.

UDDIYANA (u rgyan, o rgyan)   The country to the northwest of ancient India where Guru Rinpoche was born on a lotus flower. *See also* Orgyen.

UNCEASING VAJRA HELL (mnar med kyi dmyal ba; Skt. avichi) The lowest of the eight hot hells.

UNEXCELLED ENLIGHTENMENT (bla na med pa'i byang chub) Complete and perfect buddhahood.

UNINTERRUPTED PATH (bar chad med lam) The "path" or "basis" that is the remedy for directly eradicating the defilements that are to be abandoned on one's present path and which thereby ensures that no other interruptions can hinder the arising of the wisdom that is the result of one's particular path.

UNIVERSAL MONARCH ('khor los sgyur ba'i rgyal po; Skt. chakravartin) One who rules over the four continents of human beings. He bears the thirty-two marks of a Great Being, and is assisted in his rule by the seven precious possessions of the precious wheel, jewel, queen, minister, elephant, horse, and general.

VAIROCANA (Skt. vai ro ca na) The great Tibetan translator at the time of King Trisong Deutsen. Recognized by Padmakara as a reincarnation of an Indian pandita, he was among the first seven monks sent to India to study with Shri Singha. He is also one of the three main masters to bring the Dzogchen teachings to Tibet, the two others being Padmakara and Vimalamitra.

VAJRA (rdo rje) Literally, diamond, king of stones. As an adjective it means indestructible, invincible, firm, and so on. There is the ultimate vajra of emptiness, the conventional vajra of material substance with attributes, and the apparent symbolic or labeled vajra of the name.

VAJRA FRIEND (rdo rje grogs po) A fellow practitioner with whom one shares the sacred link of having the same master, practice, or having received teaching together.

VAJRA HOLDER (rdo rje 'dzin pa) (1) Respectful title for an accomplished master. (2) The state of enlightenment.

VAJRA MASTER (rdo rje slob dpon) A tantric master who is adept in the rituals and meaning of Vajrayana. The master from whom one receives tantric teachings. Can also refer to the master who presides over a tantric ritual.

VAJRA-LIKE SAMADHI (rdo rje lta bu'i ting nge 'dzin) The final stage of the tenth bhumi, which results in buddhahood.

VAJRADHARA (rdo rje 'chang) Vajra holder. The dharmakaya buddha of the Sarma schools. Can also refer to one's personal teacher of Vajrayana.

VAJRAYANA (rdo rje theg pa) The diamond vehicle. The practices of taking the result as the path. Same as Secret Mantra or Tantrayana.

VEHICLE (theg pa) The practice of a set of teachings that carries one to the level of fruition.

VICTORIOUS ONES (rgyal ba, jina) Same as buddhas.

VIDYADHARA (rig pa 'dzin pa) Knowledge holder. Holder (dhara) or bearer of knowledge (vidya) mantra. A realized master on one of the four stages on the tantric path of mahayoga, the tantric equivalent of the sixteen bhumis.

VIDYADHARA LEVEL OF LIFE MASTERY (tshe dbang rig 'dzin)

VIDYADHARA LEVEL OF MAHAMUDRA (phyag chen rig 'dzin)

VIDYADHARA LEVEL OF MATURATION (rnam smin rig 'dzin)

VIDYADHARA LEVEL OF SPONTANEOUS PRESENCE (lhun grub rig 'dzin)

VIDYADHARA LEVELS (rig 'dzin gyi sa) *See* Four vidyadhara levels.

VIEW (lta ba) A particular understanding and orientation based on studies of philosophy. In the context of mahamudra and trekcho, the view refers to the state of ordinary mind or self-existing wakefulness free from any concept, even of philosophical insight.

VIEW, MEDITATION, AND ACTION (lta ba sgom pa spyod pa) The philosophical orientation, the act of growing accustomed to that—usually in sitting practice—and the implementation of that insight during the activities of daily life. Each of the nine vehicles has its particular definition of view, meditation, and action.

VIPASHYANA (lhag mthong) Clear or wider seeing. Usually refers to insight into emptiness. One of the two main aspects of meditation practice, the other being shamatha.

VISHNU (khyab 'jug) "The Pervader"; as preserver of the universe, he forms part of the Hindu triad of gods, with Brahma the creator and Shiva the destroyer.

VOWS OR PRECEPTS (sdom pa) *See* Three sets of vows.

WHEEL OF GATHERING (tshogs kyi 'khor lo; Skt. ganachakra) In the ancient times, a feast assembly during which were made offerings the value of certain measures of gold. Nowadays equivalent to a feast offering (tshogs kyi mchod pa).

WISDOM DEITY (ye shes sems dpa', ye shes pa, ye shes kyi lha) The real deity abiding in dharmadhatu.

WISDOM OF PERSEVERING ACTION (bya ba nan tan gyi ye

shes) Equivalent to "all-accomplishing wisdom" (bya ba grub pa'i ye shes).

YAKSHA (gnod sbyin) A class of semidivine beings, generally beneficent but sometimes malignant. Many are local divinities of the countryside, often dwelling in sacred trees and guarding the treasure buried nearby. Others live on Mount Sumeru, guarding the realm of the gods. They are ruled by Kuvera, the god of wealth and guardian of the northern quarter.

YANGDAG (Tib. yang dag; Skt. vishuddha) One of the eight herukas of the Nyingma School. The wrathful deity of vajra mind.

YERPA (g.yer pa) A mountain retreat near Lhasa in central Tibet.

YIDAM (yi dam) A personal deity and the root of accomplishment among the three roots.

YOGA SADHANA (rnal 'byor gyi sgrub thabs) The main practice that traditionally follows the preliminaries. It includes the two stages of development and completion and is a perfect stepping-stone for approaching the more subtle practices of mahamudra and Dzogchen.

YOGIC DISCIPLINE (rtul shugs) Additional practices for a tantrika in order to train in implementing the view of Vajrayana in daily activities; for example, feast offering.

YOGI (rnal 'byor pa) Tantric practitioner.

Contact Addresses for Teachings and Retreats

For information regarding programs,
recorded and published teachings in the lineage
of Tulku Urgyen Rinpoche,
please access one of the following websites:

Shedrub Development Mandala, Nepal
WWW.SHEDRUB.NET

Rangjung Yeshe Gomdé, USA
WWW.GOMDEUSA.ORG

Rangjung Yeshe Gomdé, Denmark
WWW.GOMDE.DK

Rangjung Yeshe Publications
WWW.RANGJUNG.COM

Pundarika
WWW.PUNDARIKA.ORG